Alice-Miranda A Royal Christmas Ball

Books by Jacqueline Harvey

Kensy and Max: Breaking News
Kensy and Max: Disappearing Act
Kensy and Max: Undercover
Kensy and Max: Out of Sight
Kensy and Max: Freefall
Kensy and Max: Full Speed
Kensy and Max: Take Down
Kesny and Max: High Voltage

Alice-Miranda at School
Alice-Miranda on Holiday
Alice-Miranda Takes the Lead
Alice-Miranda at Sea
Alice-Miranda in New York
Alice-Miranda Shows the Way
Alice-Miranda in Paris
Alice-Miranda Shines Bright
Alice-Miranda in Japan
Alice-Miranda at Camp
Alice-Miranda at the Palace
Alice-Miranda in the Alps
Alice-Miranda to the Rescue
Alice-Miranda in China
Alice-Miranda Holds the Key
Alice-Miranda in Hollywood
Alice-Miranda in Scotland
Alice-Miranda Keeps the Beat
Alice-Miranda in the Outback
Alice-Miranda in Egypt

Clementine Rose and the Surprise Visitor
Clementine Rose and the Pet Day Disaster
Clementine Rose and the Perfect Present
Clementine Rose and the Farm Fiasco
Clementine Rose and the Seaside Escape
Clementine Rose and the Treasure Box
Clementine Rose and the Famous Friend
Clementine Rose and the Ballet Break-In
Clementine Rose and the Movie Magic
Clementine Rose and the Birthday Emergency
Clementine Rose and the Special Promise
Clementine Rose and the Paris Puzzle
Clementine Rose and the Wedding Wobbles
Clementine Rose and the Bake-Off Dilemma
Clementine Rose and the Best News Yet

Alice-Miranda A Royal Christmas Ball

The Official Movie Script

Alice-Miranda: A Royal Christmas Ball
is an SLR Productions Picture

PUFFIN BOOKS

PUFFIN BOOKS

UK | USA | Canada | Ireland | AustraliaIndia | New Zealand | South Africa | China

Penguin Random House Australia is part of the Penguin Random House group of companies whose addresses can be found at global.penguinrandomhouse.com.

First published by Puffin Books, an imprint of Penguin Random House Australia Pty Ltd, in 2021

Cover design by Rebecca King © Penguin Random House Australia, based on film art by SLR Productions
Internal design by Midland Typesetters, Australia

Printed and bound in Australia by Griffin Press, part of Ovato, an accredited ISO AS/NZS 14001 Environmental Management Systems printer

A catalogue record for this book is available from the National Library of Australia

ISBN 978 1 76 089746 8

Penguin Random House Australia uses papers that are natural and recyclable products, made from wood grown in sustainable forests. The logging and manufacture processes are expected to conform to the environmental regulations of the country of origin.

penguin.com.au

Every effort has been made to ensure the script that follows is accurate to the final film, however there may be small inconsistencies.

ACT
1

SCENE 1: EXT. WINCHESTERFIELD-DOWNSFORDVALE SCHOOL – MORNING

A currawong soars over the idyllic Winchesterfield-Downsfordvale school, as tyres <CRUNCH> on gravel and the school car pulls up.

We ZOOM off with the currawong towards the stables . . .

SCENE 2: EXT. SCHOOL STABLES – MORNING

. . . where it skims past ALICE-MIRANDA, in her sailor suit with a wheelie suitcase by her side. The currawong lands with a <WHISTLE> on a branch near ALICE-MIRANDA, who is farewelling her pony. ALICE-MIRANDA strokes BONAPARTE.

ALICE-MIRANDA

Bony, you won't be lonely while I'm away – you have the other ponies to keep you company.

Pan over to STUMPS, CHOPS and BUTTERCUP nearby. BONAPARTE is dismayed.

BONAPARTE

What, you're leaving me behind?

Off screen, we hear a car <HONKING>.

ALICE-MIRANDA

Sorry, Bony, I'm late!

ALICE-MIRANDA hugs BONAPARTE and ducks to grab her suitcase handle. As she rises, BONAPARTE nips her hair.

ALICE-MIRANDA (CONT'D)

Ow! Bony, why are you so naughty?

BONAPARTE

(whinnying)

Born that way.

ALICE-MIRANDA hurries from the stables, dragging her suitcase.

SCENE 3: EXT. WINCHESTERFIELD-DOWNSFORDVALE GROUNDS – MORNING

In a MONTAGE, ALICE-MIRANDA hurries past (still dragging her suitcase) and waves at:
– MRS SMITH in the kitchen baking brownies.
– CHARLIE planting seedlings.
– ASHIMA, IVORY and SUSANNAH strolling across the grounds in their school uniforms.

IVORY

See you, Alice-Miranda!

ASHIMA/SUSANNAH

Have a great break!/Miss you already!

ALICE-MIRANDA

Thanks!

ALICE-MIRANDA hurries off.

SCENE 4: EXT. WINCHESTERFIELD-DOWNSFORDVALE DRIVEWAY – MORNING

ALICE-MIRANDA dashes into the driveway and sees the school car idling with MISS HIGGINS in the driver's seat. The boot is open. MISS HIGGINS waves.

MILLIE pops her head out one back window.

MILLIE

Alice-Miranda, hurry up –

JACINTA pops her head out the other.

JACINTA

Or we'll miss the ship!

ALICE-MIRANDA heaves her suitcase into the boot, and leaps into the car. The door <SLAMS>. The car takes off.

DISSOLVE TO:

SCENE 5: INT/EXT. CAR/HARBOUR BRIDGE/OPERA HOUSE/CIRCULAR QUAY – DAY

ALICE-MIRANDA is by the window, beside MILLIE and JACINTA, as the car drives.

JACINTA
How great is this? We're missing school to go on a cruise –

MILLIE
And we're meeting the Queen! I cannot believe you know royalty, Alice-Miranda!

ALICE-MIRANDA
Well, Aunty Gee is my grandmother's best friend. You'll love her.

As they drive, we see flashes of Sydney's iconic harbour, Harbour Bridge and Opera House.

ALICE-MIRANDA gazes out the window, transfixed.

ALICE-MIRANDA (CONT'D)

The Opera House!

JACINTA

Oh, and the Sydney Harbour Bridge!

MILLIE

I can't wait for your birthday par– ow!

JACINTA has kicked MILLIE. Now she glares at her and holds a finger to her lips.

JACINTA

(whispering)

Shh.

MILLIE grimaces – oops. She forgot. Luckily, ALICE-MIRANDA is too busy staring out the window to notice. The car pulls up.

MISS HIGGINS (O.S.)

Just look at that ship!

The girls look out the window at the ship – then at each other in excitement.

ALICE-MIRANDA/MILLIE/JACINTA
(squealing)

As the car doors open . . .

ALICE-MIRANDA
Thanks for the lift, Miss Higgins.

MISS HIGGINS waves.

MISS HIGGINS
Enjoy yourselves, girls.

DISSOLVE TO:

SCENE 6: EXT. DOCKS/GANGPLANK/ CORRIDOR – CONTINUOUS – DAY

The girls stand with their bags gaping up at the ship.

MILLIE

(reading)

The Queen Georgiana. So the ship's named after your Aunty Gee?

ALICE-MIRANDA

Yes, and it's the ship's maiden voyage – its first ever trip.

Behind them, a BODYGUARD strides towards the gangplank, followed by a small, stout woman (QUEEN GEORGIANA/AUNTY GEE) in a caftan, large straw hat and sunglasses. She's being escorted by a dapper man in a straw hat (LORD LLOYD LANCASTER-BROWN).

LLOYD

Take care, Aunty. Ships can be dangerous and we don't want a tumble.

AUNTY GEE

Don't be silly, Lloyd. These legs have held me up for 70 years! They're hardly going to fail now.

A little behind them is a wiry woman in black clutching a folder of documents. It's MARJORIE, AUNTY GEE'S head of security. She mutters into her smart watch.

AUNTY GEE passes behind the girls, then stops in delight.

AUNTY GEE (O.S.)
Alice-Miranda!

ALICE-MIRANDA, JACINTA and MILLIE turn.

ALICE-MIRANDA
Aunty Gee!

AUNTY GEE scoops ALICE-MIRANDA into a hug, then beams at MILLIE and JACINTA, as MARJORIE, LLOYD and the BODYGUARD hover behind her. MILLIE gapes in awe.

MILLIE
(loudly)
You're the Queen!

MARJORIE glares at MILLIE, who flushes.

MILLIE (CONT'D)

Oops.

MARJORIE turns to AUNTY GEE.

MARJORIE

(undertone)

Your Majesty, you're supposed to be undercover.

AUNTY GEE snorts.

AUNTY GEE

(to the girls)

This is Marjorie, my head of security. She's a weeny bit tense.

(to MARJORIE)

Can't I just be normal for a bit?

MARJORIE winces.

MARJORIE

Your Majesty, you're not normal.

She nods to the folder she's holding. CLOSE ON the small royal crest on the cover.

MARJORIE (CONT'D)

Since you insisted on coming on this cruise – against my advice – you must be careful.

AUNTY GEE

Heavens, Marjorie, no one notices an old lady saying hello to a friend.

She gestures around at the busy dock. She's right, no one has noticed. MARJORIE frowns, not convinced.

MARJORIE

We can't be sure. Particularly with the threatening messages you're receiving.

AUNTY GEE

A few emails. So what?

MARJORIE scrolls on her watch.

MARJORIE

Here's today's.

MARJORIE (CONT'D)

(reading)

'We have eyes everywhere. Prepare to kiss your Queen goodbye!' Then there's the nasty headlines.

AUNTY GEE scoffs.

AUNTY GEE

Oh, newspapers!

MARJORIE

'Careless Cruise Queen'. The story says you're getting sloppy, displaying your priceless jewels on a ship. I want to know who's planting these stories.

AUNTY GEE

The papers have to print something. I'm just today's story.

At this point, LLOYD steps in, sweeps off his hat and bows dashingly to the girls.

LLOYD

I'm Lord Lloyd Lancaster-Brown, the Queen's nephew. And this is my fiancé, Marjorie.

(to MARJORIE)

Darling, relax! You'd think a couple of girls excited to see the Queen were international spies.

MARJORIE blushes, flustered.

LLOYD puts his arm out and AUNTY GEE takes it, nodding. He holds his other arm out. Reluctantly, MARJORIE takes it.

LLOYD (CONT'D)

Come on ladies, there's fun to be had. But watch your step, Your Majesty.

LLOYD winks at the girls. As they board the ship, MARJORIE frowns suspiciously back at the girls.

The girls pick up their suitcase handles and trundle them towards the gangplank.

MILLIE
Lord Lloyd seems nice, but I have no idea why he's marrying her.

ALICE-MIRANDA shrugs.

ALICE-MIRANDA
Aunty Gee isn't easy to manage. Keeping her safe would make anyone anxious!

The girls giggle. As they join the boarding queue, ALICE-MIRANDA glances up . . .

ALICE-MIRANDA (CONT'D)
There's Mum and Dad! And Granny Valentina and Aunt Charlotte.

HUGH and CECELIA, GRANNY VALENTINA (in caftan with jewellery) and AUNT CHARLOTTE are onboard, waving. As ALICE-MIRANDA speaks, we ZOOM IN on each person.

As ALICE-MIRANDA waves back, JACINTA nudges MILLIE. In front of the girls, devilishly-handsome twin boys (the PRINCES) are going up the gangplank with their suitcases.

JACINTA
(to MILLIE)
Those boys look exactly the same.

Together, the boys turn.

PRINCE EDGAR
That's because we're identical twins, genius.

Both PRINCES laugh and walk onto the ship. ALICE-MIRANDA picks up her bag, then notices JACINTA rolling her eyes.

ALICE-MIRANDA
What's wrong?

JACINTA
(whispering)
Those boys were totally rude.

They follow the boys up the gangplank. From behind, ALICE-MIRANDA can't see the boy's faces but spots their suitcases with stickers all over them. CLOSE ON the royal crest on one of the suitcases.

ALICE-MIRANDA
(whispering)
See the royal crest? They're Aunty Gee's grandsons, the princes.

As the boys turn down a corridor, MILLIE and JACINTA gape.

JACINTA
They're princes?! They weren't acting very royal!

ALICE-MIRANDA continues down the corridor and the girls follow. MILLIE examines a number on a door. She stops, pulls out a key card and sticks it in the slot. The light flashes red.

ALICE-MIRANDA
Oops, wrong room. I think it's down there.

She points down the hall and they trundle to another door. MILLIE tries the card and the light goes green.

<u>SCENE 7: INT. CRUISE SHIP – CABIN – DAY</u>

MILLIE opens the cabin door then bars the way in with a grin.

MILLIE

Password.

JACINTA and ALICE-MIRANDA look at each other, perplexed.

ALICE-MIRANDA

Um . . . ships and chips?

MILLIE smiles.

MILLIE

Nope.

JACINTA peeps over MILLIE'S shoulder into the room.

JACINTA

(impressed)

Whoa!

MILLIE

That's the password!

The girls giggle as they burst in and gaze around.

ALICE-MIRANDA

It's so lovely.

MILLIE picks up a pillow.

MILLIE

Pillow fight!

MILLIE <THUMPS> ALICE-MIRANDA, who grabs another pillow and <THUMPS> her back.

Just then, there's a low, long <HONK> and the ship starts to rumble. The girls drop the pillows.

ALICE-MIRANDA

We're off!

ALICE-MIRANDA runs to the sliding balcony door, followed by MILLIE, while JACINTA bounces from bed to bed to get there. The water around the ship swirls and the Opera House starts to recede behind them.

The girls look at each other and squeal. Just then, JACINTA'S mother, AMBROSIA, sticks her head in.

JACINTA

Mum, you're here!

JACINTA runs over and hugs her. Then AMBROSIA'S <RINGTONE> sounds. She looks at her phone.

AMBROSIA

Sorry, honey, got to take this.

She clamps the phone to her ear, waves at JACINTA and exits. JACINTA frowns, a little upset at her mother leaving. ALICE-MIRANDA notices and puts an arm around JACINTA.

ALICE-MIRANDA

Shall we take a look around
the ship? I'm sure we'll see your
mother later.

JACINTA nods.

JACINTA/MILLIE

Sure./Yay!

They exit, with ALICE-MIRANDA in the lead . . .

SCENE 8: INT. CRUISE SHIP – CORRIDOR – DAY

. . . But as she steps out of the door, ALICE-MIRANDA bumps into a bald staffer, PETER, who hurries along the corridor in uniform carrying a teetering pile of towels.

The towels begin to topple.

PETER

Argh!

ALICE-MIRANDA deftly catches the towels and takes the stack. She pops her head around the towels and offers one hand.

ALICE-MIRANDA

Hello, I'm Alice-Miranda Highton-

Smith-Kennington-Jones and I'm very sorry about that!

PETER doesn't take her hand and won't meet her eye.

PETER

(gruffly)

Thank you.

As JACINTA and MILLIE step into the corridor, he snatches the towels and hurries off. The girls watch.

JACINTA

What is it with the people on this ship? He's almost as rude as the princes.

MILLIE

There's something weird about his face, too.

ALICE-MIRANDA shrugs.

ALICE-MIRANDA

He can't help the way he looks,

and he's probably busy with so
many people on board.

The girls scamper down the corridor in the opposite direction to PETER.

SCENE 9: INT. CRUISE SHIP – LIBRARY – DAY

The girls peek into the library.

ALICE-MIRANDA
I didn't know cruise ships had
libraries.

As MILLIE and ALICE-MIRANDA check out the books, JACINTA opens a closed door and disappears through it.

JACINTA (O.S.)
(calling)
You've got to see this!

SCENE 10: INT. CRUISE SHIP – DRAWING ROOM – DAY

ALICE-MIRANDA and MILLIE enter.

In one corner of the shadowy room, there's a dazzling case of jewels. A roped barrier surrounds the case.

MILLIE/JACINTA

Ooh!/The Queen's crown jewels!

ALICE-MIRANDA gazes at them.

ALICE-MIRANDA

Yes, there's the royal sceptre, the orb of power and the ruby tiara. They're dazzling!

As she names them, we PAN CLOSE over the royal sceptre, the ruby tiara and the orb of power. On the orb is a tiny keyhole, barely visible.

MILLIE

The ruby in that tiara is huge.

MILLIE leans over the rope, presses her forehead against the glass to see the tiara better, and sets off the alarm.

MILLIE leaps back and the girls cover their ears in surprise as the alarm <WAILS>. MARJORIE races in . . . then halts as she sees it's just the girls.

MARJORIE presses a few buttons and the alarm stops. Crossly, she rounds on MILLIE.

MARJORIE

Wasn't the door locked? Where's the guard?

ALICE-MIRANDA steps in.

ALICE-MIRANDA

The door wasn't locked and there was no guard. We're terribly sorry.

JACINTA

Why are the crown jewels on the ship?

MARJORIE resets the alarm with crisp irritation. <BEEP! BEEP! BEEP!> Clearly, she wants the girls to leave.

ALICE-MIRANDA
Aunty Gee wanted them on display for the ship's maiden voyage.

MARJORIE
You mean, Her Majesty wanted them on display.

AUNTY GEE'S BODYGUARD enters hurriedly.

MARJORIE (CONT'D)
(crossly)
Where have you been?

BODYGUARD
Sorry, Ma'am, I needed the bathroom.

MARJORIE glares at him for a beat. He squirms. Then she turns to the girls.

MARJORIE
Run along, girls. We don't want any more false alarms.

MARJORIE frowns at MILLIE, who flushes. ALICE-MIRANDA jumps in.

ALICE-MIRANDA

Sorry, we didn't mean to cause trouble. We'd better get ready for the sunset party.

ALICE-MIRANDA leads the other girls out.

MILLIE

(muttering)

I definitely don't like her!

DISSOLVE TO:

SCENE 11: EXT. CRUISE SHIP – DECK – AFTERNOON

A WAITER sets a table with forks, spoons and a host of tumblers as the sun drops over the ocean.

Behind the table, the sun drops lower and begins to turn pink as it sets.

TRANSITION TO:

SCENE 12: EXT. CRUISE SHIP – DECK – SUNSET

The same table, but now it's got an ice cream service on it, the sun has set and guests are milling about.

The girls slip onto the deck in delight.

JACINTA

Ice cream, a cruise and my BFFs. Best day ever!

MILLIE

And it's your birthday tomorrow, Alice-Miranda.

ALICE-MIRANDA

I can't wait!

They link arms and share a smile. Then ALICE-MIRANDA notices something. She nudges JACINTA.

ALICE-MIRANDA (CONT'D)

Jacinta, Lucas is waving at us.

JACINTA looks and blushes as LUCAS waves.

JACINTA

Oh my goodness, I didn't know Lucas was coming!

MILLIE

And there's his dad, Lawrence Ridley, the movie star.

ALICE-MIRANDA

Someone's introduced him to Aunt Charlotte.

On LAWRENCE RIDLEY, who is chatting with AUNT CHARLOTTE. He is admiring her emerald and gold bird-shaped earrings.

LAWRENCE

What unusual earrings. They look lovely on you.

AUNT CHARLOTTE touches her ear and smiles.

AUNT CHARLOTTE

Why, thank you. My niece chose them for me.

MILLIE

Lucas looks just like his dad doesn't he? Super handsome.

MILLIE nudges JACINTA, who blushes.

ALICE-MIRANDA

There's Granny with Aunty Gee.

The two elderly ladies are finishing a song.

AUNTY GEE/GRANNY VALENTINA

(singing)

And so we meet again . . .

They break into a snorting laugh.

MILLIE

I hope we stay friends all our lives like them.

ALICE-MIRANDA, JACINTA and MILLIE look between themselves.

ALICE-MIRANDA/MILLIE/JACINTA

We will!

They burst into laughter.

LUCAS arrives balancing three ice cream cones. He hands one to ALICE-MIRANDA, one to MILLIE . . .

ALICE-MIRANDA/MILLIE

Lucas, thanks!/Thanks!

Then turns to JACINTA and hands her a pink ice cream cone.

LUCAS

Hi Alice-Miranda, hi Millie.
Hi Jacinta – strawberry's your
favourite, right?

JACINTA nods. She's swooning and embarrassed and trying to play it cool, all at once.

JACINTA

Um . . . thanks.

A pause where JACINTA and LUCAS smile shyly at each other, and MILLIE nudges ALICE-MIRANDA. ALICE-MIRANDA smiles, then interrupts.

ALICE-MIRANDA

I didn't know your dad was coming, Lucas.

LUCAS snaps out of it and turns to ALICE-MIRANDA.

LUCAS

He's about to shoot a movie in the Australian outback and he wanted to see me before it started.

ALICE-MIRANDA spots her parents.

ALICE-MIRANDA

There's Mum by the table. Millie, can you mind my ice cream?

She passes MILLIE her cone and ducks off, but is blocked by AUNT CHARLOTTE who bites into a cookie then gags.

AUNT CHARLOTTE

Bleurgh!

ALICE-MIRANDA

Excuse me, Aunt Charlotte!

But AUNT CHARLOTTE has turned to LAWRENCE as he's biting into his cookie.

AUNT CHARLOTTE

Don't eat that!

Too late – LAWRENCE has already bitten.

LAWRENCE

Bleurgh! These are disgusting.

LAWRENCE looks around, trying to find a waiter.

ALICE-MIRANDA ducks around them and reaches the table. CECELIA is nowhere in sight.

Then she spies the tablecloth twitching. She lifts the cloth and peeks underneath.

SCENE 13: EXT. CRUISE SHIP – DECK/ UNDER THE TABLE – SUNSET

The PRINCES are sniggering under the table as they sandwich chocolate cookies together with a tube of fish paste to make fake sandwich cookies.

PRINCE LOUIS

Yum, yum, choc-fish biscuits!
Delicious!

The PRINCES snigger. ALICE-MIRANDA slips under, surprising them. She sticks her hand out.

ALICE-MIRANDA

Hello, I'm Alice-Miranda.

The boys ignore her outstretched hand.

PRINCE EDGAR

Who invited you?

ALICE-MIRANDA ignores the rudeness.

ALICE-MIRANDA

Are you putting those on the table as a prank?

She points to the doctored cookies.

PRINCE LOUIS

Duh, of course. It's a joke.

ALICE-MIRANDA tilts her head.

ALICE-MIRANDA

But jokes are meant to make people laugh and this one probably won't.

The PRINCES share a look – what a killjoy! Suddenly, they get it.

PRINCE EDGAR

Oh. You're that goody-goody Granny's always going on about.

AMBROSIA (O.S.)

Yech! What is this?

The PRINCES high-five.

PRINCE LOUIS

Anchovy paste works its fishy magic.

ALICE-MIRANDA is crawling out backwards as the tablecloth flaps – MARJORIE has lifted it.

Multiple disgusted faces stare at the PRINCES – one with the cookies, the other with the tube of fish paste. AUNTY GEE'S face looms into view.

AUNTY GEE

(sternly)

I think you boys owe everyone an apology.

ALICE-MIRANDA stands. MILLIE stands by AUNTY GEE, still clutching ALICE-MIRANDA'S drippy ice cream cone. The PRINCES also climb out into view.

PRINCE EDGAR/PRINCE LOUIS

(muffled)

Whoops. Sorry./Yeah . . .

AUNTY GEE

I agreed to have my grandsons stay and attend Fayle School for Boys next term, to give them more experience of the world. Perhaps I made the wrong decision.

ALICE-MIRANDA

Oh, I don't think so. Our friend Lucas goes to Fayle and he loves it.

AUNTY GEE arches an eyebrow.

AUNTY GEE

Maybe Lucas can teach them some manners. Lloyd went there too, and raves about it. He was the head of the drama club in his day.

AUNTY GEE turns to the PRINCES.

AUNTY GEE (CONT'D)

Both of you, off to your room.

PRINCE LOUIS

But we didn't get any ice cream!

AUNTY GEE glares and they slink out. When they're gone, AUNTY GEE sits heavily on a chair as if she's exhausted.

AUNTY GEE
They wear me out. I'm too old.

MILLIE
You're not too old, Aunty Gee.

ALICE-MIRANDA (O.S.)
Here's something to cheer you up.

ALICE-MIRANDA hands AUNTY GEE a fresh ice cream cone.

AUNTY GEE
Vanilla with sprinkles –
my favourite. Thank you,
Alice-Miranda!

ALICE-MIRANDA sits beside AUNTY GEE. MILLIE offers ALICE-MIRANDA her melted, now flattened ice cream cone.

MILLIE
And this is yours, Alice-Miranda.

Everyone looks at the flattened cone.

MILLIE (CONT'D)

I had to take a few licks to stop it dripping.

ALICE-MIRANDA smiles.

ALICE-MIRANDA

I might grab a fresh one.

Everyone laughs.

We RISE over the deck as the sky darkens to night and the thin crescent moon rises over the ocean. <MUSIC> plays, everyone is dancing and chatting. They're having a blast!

CUT TO:

SCENE 14: INT. CRUISE SHIP – CORRIDOR – LATER THAT NIGHT

A happy GRANNY VALENTINA does a quickstep dance down the corridor, singing to herself.

GRANNY VALENTINA

(warbling song)

She finds her cabin door. She opens it with her key card. The light flashes green. She enters.

SCENE 15: INT. CRUISE SHIP – CABIN – LATER THAT NIGHT

GRANNY VALENTINA stops dead. Her room has been ransacked! She hurries to the dresser. Her jewellery box is empty.

GRANNY VALENTINA

My jewellery!

Inside the box she finds a small yellow note. She picks it up and unfurls it.

As she reads it, she sits down on her bed, aghast.

GRANNY VALENTINA (CONT'D)

Oh dear . . .

DISSOLVE TO:

SCENE 16: INT. CRUISE SHIP – CABIN – MORNING

The next morning ALICE-MIRANDA sits bolt upright in her bed, excited. She crawls to the end of her bed and sees two presents, one big and one small.

ALICE-MIRANDA
Thanks, Mum and Dad!

Then the presents slide sideways and <THUD> against the wall.

ALICE-MIRANDA (CONT'D)
Whoa!

ALICE-MIRANDA almost loses her balance and bounces back on the bed.

ALICE-MIRANDA (CONT'D)
Better leave them for later.

She peeks out the curtains. The sky is stormy, the sea is grey with big waves and the ship is lurching.

ALICE-MIRANDA (CONT'D)
A storm!

She turns to see JACINTA sit up in bed, swaying and looking green. She flops back down again.

JACINTA
Ugh, I don't feel well.

MILLIE
(groaning)
Me either.

ALICE-MIRANDA kneels by their beds.

ALICE-MIRANDA
You poor things, you must have seasickness. I'll find you something.

She hops up and disappears out the cabin door. When she's gone, MILLIE pops up her head.

MILLIE
(whispering)
What about Alice-Miranda's

surprise party? We're supposed to organize that today! But I'm so sick!

JACINTA
(whispering)
Let's hope Aunty Gee has it under control. Ugh, I'm going to –

JACINTA falls out of bed and stumbles into the bathroom, <SLAMMING> the door behind her.

Just then, ALICE-MIRANDA arrives back with full water bottles and packets of crackers.

ALICE-MIRANDA
These should help.

ALICE-MIRANDA picks up her teddy bear, Brummel, and tucks him in beside MILLIE.

ALICE-MIRANDA (CONT'D)
Brummel will look after you both until I get back. I'd better check if Mum and Dad are alright.

As ALICE-MIRANDA finds her clothes, MILLIE hugs Brummel to her chest and groans.

MILLIE

Oh, Brummel!

SCENE 17: INT. CRUISE SHIP – CORRIDOR – DAY

ALICE-MIRANDA, now dressed, peeks her head out of her door. The corridor is deserted.

ALICE-MIRANDA steps out into the corridor and skips along it.

PETER, the bald staffer, enters the far end of the corridor pushing a low, platform trolley with white laundry bags on it.

ALICE-MIRANDA waves but PETER doesn't respond. As they approach, PETER steers the trolley one way and ALICE-MIRANDA smiles and moves the other way so they can pass.

ALICE-MIRANDA
Lots of people must be seasick today.

Just then, the boat pitches and they lurch the same way.

ALICE-MIRANDA (CONT'D)
Whoa!

ALICE-MIRANDA lands among the white laundry bags in the platform-trolley, which make a <JANGLING> sound. PETER looms over her, annoyed, as she sits up.

ALICE-MIRANDA (CONT'D)
We must stop bumping into each other this way.

ALICE-MIRANDA notices PETER isn't smiling and still won't meet her eyes. This guy is a tough nut to crack.

PETER
(gruffly)
I've got laundry to fetch.

ALICE-MIRANDA hops off the trolley, and PETER hurries away pushing the trolley.

ALICE-MIRANDA walks on. She turns the corner, bumping into PRINCE EDGAR, who is green and staggering along clutching two bottles of water.

ALICE-MIRANDA

Are you seasick, too? I'm so sorry. Can I help?

PRINCE EDGAR

(groaning)

Exactly who I wanted to meet. Not.

(calling)

Louis, I'm coming!

PRINCE LOUIS (O.S.)

Ugh, I feel terrible.

Edgar pulls out his key card, falls through his door and <SLAMS> it behind him. ALICE-MIRANDA skips off.

SCENE 18: EXT. CRUISE SHIP – DECK – DAY/AFTERNOON

The deck is bleak, deserted and windswept. Rain pelts the floor. Then the rain gets lighter.

P.A. SYSTEM (O.S.)
This is your Captain speaking. We're passing through the storm and will soon be out the other side . . .

The clouds part and the rain stops. The sun peeks out. One guest arrives and takes a deck chair. As the clouds roll away, more guests slowly arrive.

SCENE 19: EXT. CRUISE SHIP – DECK – LATE AFTERNOON

The weather is perfect. The sun is setting. ALICE-MIRANDA wanders along the deck, crunching an apple.

AUNTY GEE and GRANNY VALENTINA are carrying bags of flowers. When they see ALICE-MIRANDA, they put the bags of flowers down and stand in front of them to hide them.

GRANNY VALENTINA
Happy birthday, Alice-Miranda.

AUNTY GEE
Happy birthday! What have you been up to with so many people seasick?

ALICE-MIRANDA
I had breakfast with my parents.

QUICK CUT CLOSE ON ALICE-MIRANDA sitting between her parents in the dining room.

ALICE-MIRANDA (CONT'D)
Then I went for a swim and I had the pool all to myself except for the lifeguard.

QUICK CUT CLOSE ON ALICE-MIRANDA'S blissed-out face, hair rippling in the water, as she floats on her back in the pool.

ALICE-MIRANDA (CONT'D)
Then I went tenpin bowling

by myself and the swaying ship
helped me get three strikes!

QUICK CUT CLOSE ON ALICE-MIRANDA'S face, watching in anticipation. We hear a strike with pins falling. <CRASH! CRASH! CRASH!> Her eyes widen and she beams.

ALICE-MIRANDA (CONT'D)
And then I went to a movie. Did
you know there's a cinema on this
ship? I sat right in the middle.

QUICK CUT CLOSE ON ALICE-MIRANDA'S face, light flickering over it, as she watches a movie in an empty cinema.

GRANNY VALENTINA
Wonderful! You did so much in
one day.

ALICE-MIRANDA
I think I'll check on Millie and
Jacinta now.

ALICE-MIRANDA skips off as AUNTY GEE

and GRANNY VALENTINA shake their heads in wonder.

AUNTY GEE
That granddaughter of yours
is perpetually positive.

ALICE-MIRANDA skips past LAWRENCE RIDLEY and AUNT CHARLOTTE talking in deck-chairs, then AMBROSIA in a hat and sunglasses, still deep in conversation on her phone.

SCENE 20: INT. CRUISE SHIP – CORRIDOR – LATE AFTERNOON

AUNT CHARLOTTE, HUGH and CECELIA return to their cabins along the corridor together.

CECELIA
We'd better hurry to get the party
ready.

AUNT CHARLOTTE opens her door with her key card.

HUGH and CECELIA do the same.

SCENE 21: INT. CRUISE SHIP – CABIN – LATE AFTERNOON

JACINTA and MILLIE are getting dressed for dinner.

JACINTA

They said to keep her busy for ten more minutes until they're ready.

MILLIE

That can't be too hard.

They nod at each other. Just then, ALICE-MIRANDA enters.

ALICE-MIRANDA

Wonderful, you're feeling better?

JACINTA

So much better.

ALICE-MIRANDA

Great, I had so much fun I forgot to have lunch. Let's go eat!

MILLIE and JACINTA share a worried look.

JACINTA

Maybe . . . you should open your presents first!

She points to the presents at the end of ALICE-MIRANDA'S bed. ALICE-MIRANDA gazes at them.

ALICE-MIRANDA

They can wait until after dinner. I'm starving.

MILLIE points to the crackers ALICE-MIRANDA left on her bedside table.

MILLIE

How about a delicious cracker? So healthy and tasty, yum yum!

Puzzled, ALICE-MIRANDA tilts her head.

ALICE-MIRANDA

Thanks, that's kind, but I'd rather have a proper meal.

ALICE-MIRANDA exits. JACINTA and MILLIE trail slowly after her, sharing a panicked look. This isn't going to plan.

<u>SCENE 22: INT. CRUISE SHIP – CABIN – LATE AFTERNOON</u>

HUGH is putting on his jacket in the mirror. CECELIA, dressed for dinner, sits on the bed and opens her bedside table drawer. It's empty.

CECELIA

Hugh, did you move my jewellery box?

HUGH

(frowns)

No?

CECELIA

It's gone!

HUGH opens his bedside table drawer.

HUGH

My watch is gone too! We've been robbed.

CECELIA

Wait. Look at this.

She pulls a small yellow note from her drawer. The pair huddle over it and read it. They look at each other in dismay.

SCENE 23: INT. CRUISE SHIP – CABIN – EVENING

In another cabin, AUNT CHARLOTTE searches through her purse for her emerald earrings.

AUNT CHARLOTTE

I'm sure I put my earrings in here.

She pulls out an identical yellow note and reads it in shock.

SCENE 24: INT. CRUISE SHIP – CORRIDOR – EVENING

ALICE-MIRANDA is walking with purpose towards the dining room. MILLIE and JACINTA linger behind her.

JACINTA

(whispering to MILLIE)

How can we slow her down? She's unstoppable!

MILLIE

(whispering)

I know.

(loudly)

Look out this window, Alice-Miranda.

JACINTA and MILLIE stand by a window and gesture. Outside, it's pitch black.

JACINTA

Yes, isn't the ocean beautiful from here? So . . . mysterious.

ALICE-MIRANDA takes a few steps back and gazes out the window, puzzled.

ALICE-MIRANDA

Yes . . . but it's hard to see anything at night. I'll take a look in the morning.

She hurries off. MILLIE and JACINTA share a despairing look.

SCENE 25: INT. CRUISE SHIP – DECK – EVENING

Everyone is gathered on the deck, getting ready – LUCAS is blowing balloons, LLOYD is looking green and seasick and MARJORIE is watching AUNTY GEE.

AUNTY GEE and GRANNY VALENTINA are decorating ALICE-MIRANDA'S chair with flowers from the bags to make a flowery throne. They step back to take a look.

GRANNY VALENTINA

Lovely!

As CECELIA and HUGH position a massive string of streamers above where LUCAS is blowing up balloons, ALICE-MIRANDA walks in.

She stops dead, truly surprised.

ALICE-MIRANDA

Oh!

Her parents drop the streamers. They drift over LUCAS'S head.

EVERYONE

(in a muddle)

Surprise!/Surprise!

LUCAS fights his way out of the streamers a second too late.

LUCAS

Wait, surprise!

ALICE-MIRANDA blushes, embarrassed.

ALICE-MIRANDA

Thank you, everyone! I really had no idea!

MILLIE and JACINTA shrug.

MILLIE

We tried our best.

ALICE-MIRANDA hugs her parents.

AUNTY GEE

And here's your birthday throne.

AUNTY GEE shows ALICE-MIRANDA to the flowery throne. ALICE-MIRANDA hesitates.

ALICE-MIRANDA

Isn't the Queen supposed to sit first?

AUNTY GEE

Not on your birthday.

ALICE-MIRANDA sits and AUNTY GEE sits beside her. MILLIE and JACINTA sit on ALICE-MIRANDA'S other side. LLOYD wobbles past.

LLOYD

Happy birthday. I'm afraid I'm
feeling unwell and must retire.

As he stumbles off, MILLIE leans over.

MILLIE

(whispering)

I know how he feels

AUNTY GEE

(calling out)

Hugh, what's the time? Our guest of honour is ready to eat.

HUGH starts to check his wrist, remembers his stolen watch and the note.

HUGH

(hesitating)

I must have left my watch in my cabin.

AUNTY GEE

Lawrence?

LAWRENCE grimaces.

LAWRENCE

Unfortunately I've forgotten my watch too, Your Majesty.

AUNTY GEE

That's unlucky.

Then a waiter arrives bearing plates.

AUNTY GEE (CONT'D)

Oh, here it comes.

As dinner is served, ALICE-MIRANDA looks around. Everyone is eating. No one is chatting and everyone looks worried. Only the <SCRAPES> of cutlery on plates can be heard.

ALICE-MIRANDA

(whispering)

Is it me or is everyone very quiet?

MILLIE

(whispering)

Maybe they're still feeling seasick.

ALICE-MIRANDA nods but doesn't seem convinced.

ALICE-MIRANDA

Maybe.

MILLIE notices the key necklace around AUNTY GEE'S neck.

MILLIE

Aunty Gee, no offense but your necklace is quite plain. You must have fancier things. After all, you are the Queen!

AUNTY GEE laughs.

AUNTY GEE

Being a true Queen isn't about necklaces and tiaras, Millie. It's about duty and character.

ALICE-MIRANDA smiles at AUNTY GEE.

ALICE-MIRANDA

I like your necklace. Where did you get it?

AUNTY GEE

My father, the King, gave it to me on my tenth birthday. He said it was

the key to the monarchy and taught
me a little riddle to go with it.

MILLIE
What was the riddle?

AUNTY GEE thinks hard, then recites:

AUNTY GEE
'If royal trouble comes to be,
the proof is under lock and key.'
I think that's how it went.

JACINTA
Mysterious!

ALICE-MIRANDA
I wonder what it means?

AUNTY GEE shrugs. She doesn't know.

AUNTY GEE
I think he just made it up for
fun. Daddy was rather like my
grandsons; loved riddles and tricks.

Still, it's the only piece of jewellery
I never take off.

CLOSE ON ALICE-MIRANDA as that word makes her eyes widen.

ALICE-MIRANDA
(whispering)
Jewellery . . .

She gazes at CECELIA. CLOSE ON CECELIA'S bare neck.

ALICE-MIRANDA (CONT'D)
(to herself)
Where's Mum's necklace?

She turns to AUNT CHARLOTTE. CLOSE ON her bare ears.

ALICE-MIRANDA (CONT'D)
(to herself)
And Aunt Charlotte's bird
earrings? She loves them . . .

She turns to her father . . .

ALICE-MIRANDA (CONT'D)
(to herself)
Daddy and Lawrence couldn't tell Aunty Gee the time. Where are their watches?

CLOSE ON HUGH'S bare wrist, then LAWRENCE'S bare wrist. ALICE-MIRANDA turns to MILLIE and JACINTA.

ALICE-MIRANDA (CONT'D)
(whispering)
Have you noticed no one's wearing jewellery or watches?

JACINTA and MILLIE glance around. CLOSE ON bare necks, bare arms, bare ears, bare wrists.

JACINTA
(whispering)
You're right. Maybe they've been stolen?

The three girls share a shocked glance.

ALICE-MIRANDA
(whispering)
But then why isn't anyone saying anything? And why haven't they told the captain?

Then AMBROSIA bursts in, upset.

AMBROSIA
(loudly)
I've been on an important call all afternoon and just got back to my cabin. Someone stole my jewellery and is trying to blackmail me!

GUESTS
(gasping)

ALICE-MIRANDA'S eyes widen as AMBROSIA produces a little yellow note and reads it.

AMBROSIA
(reading)
'Say anything about your jewellery and kiss your Queen goodbye!'

GUESTS
(gasping again)

AUNTY GEE reels. MARJORIE springs up and hurries to AMBROSIA. AMBROSIA hands her the note. HUGH stands.

HUGH
Now it's out, I think anyone who
has a note should speak up.

He produces a yellow note from his pocket. Half of the guests hold up yellow notes.

On high alert, MARJORIE mutters into her watch.

In a flash, the BODYGUARD slips in and stands by AUNTY GEE.

MARJORIE crouches beside AUNTY GEE and shows her HUGH'S little yellow note. ALICE-MIRANDA, sitting beside AUNTY GEE, watches and listens closely.

AUNTY GEE
Could it be the princes?

(calling)

Boys! Come here! Is this another one of your pranks?

The PRINCES are shocked.

PRINCE EDGAR

No way, Granny!

CLOSE ON ALICE-MIRANDA as she twirls her hair and narrows her eyes.

FLASHBACK to Edgar wobbling along the corridor with the water bottles.

ALICE-MIRANDA

(quietly)

Sorry to interrupt, Aunty Gee, but I don't think it can be them. The princes were very seasick today.

The PRINCES hear this and look at ALICE-MIRANDA, reassessing her. Perhaps she's okay.

MARJORIE is irritated at the conversation being taken over by a child, but keeps her cool.

MARJORIE
(low voice)
She's probably right, Your Majesty. The wording is worryingly similar to the emails.

AUNTY GEE waves the boys away and they return to their seats.

AUNTY GEE
So you think it's the same person who sent the emails?

MARJORIE nods and AUNTY GEE slumps.

AUNTY GEE (CONT'D)
Marjorie, I'm sorry. I've not taken the threats seriously enough.

ALICE-MIRANDA has been watching this. She gestures to the girls to follow her.

GUESTS
(murmuring, speculating)

ALICE-MIRANDA, MILLIE and JACINTA slip out.

SCENE 26: INT. CRUISE SHIP – LIBRARY – NIGHT

The girls sit on the floor.

ALICE-MIRANDA
We need to think.

Just then, LUCAS enters the room.

LUCAS
I saw you slip out. What's going on?

JACINTA moves over to make room and he sits.

ALICE-MIRANDA
The thief has to be on the ship
with us –

JACINTA shudders.

JACINTA
Creepy!

ALICE-MIRANDA
And it's definitely not the princes
playing a prank.

LUCAS

Why are you so sure? Maybe they were faking being seasick?

ALICE-MIRANDA

Because . . .

CLOSE ON ALICE-MIRANDA as she remembers.

FLASHBACK to MILLIE getting the wrong room with the key card and the red flashing light. ALICE-MIRANDA'S eyes widen.

ALICE-MIRANDA (CONT'D)

. . . because it has to be someone who has one of these to get into every room!

ALICE-MIRANDA pulls out her key card.

MILLIE

That means –

ALICE-MIRANDA

Someone who works on the ship . . .

Then MILLIE freezes. She's heard something. She puts her finger to her lips and points to the next room. Frozen still, the kids hear <BEEP! BEEP! BEEP! BEEP!>.

Someone is opening the jewellery cabinet with the code in the next room – they can hear the familiar sound the code-pad makes.

In silence, JACINTA covers her mouth. MILLIE hunches over. LUCAS'S eyes are wide. Only ALICE-MIRANDA keeps her cool. She stands slowly and silently creeps to the door to the next room.

Then the bald porter PETER hurries in carrying a loaded white laundry bag over his shoulder, like a sack. In his other hand is the glittering royal sceptre.

For the third time, he bumps into ALICE-MIRANDA. PETER and ALICE-MIRANDA gape at each other in shock.

ALICE-MIRANDA/PETER

You?/You!

ALICE-MIRANDA looks from the bag of jewellery in one hand, to the sceptre in his other. PETER suddenly bolts out the opposite door.

ALICE-MIRANDA

Don't let him get away!

ALICE-MIRANDA follows in hot pursuit with the kids racing out after her.

SCENE 27: INT. CRUISE SHIP – CORRIDORS – NIGHT

The chase is on through the corridors! LUCAS stumbles –

LUCAS

Ow!

– and ALICE-MIRANDA and JACINTA stop to help him up.

MILLIE is now in the lead. ALICE-MIRANDA sprints after her, followed by JACINTA and LUCAS.

PETER slips past a trolley with ALICE-MIRANDA'S enormous birthday cake on it. MILLIE is right behind him.

ALICE-MIRANDA
(calling)
Use the trolley, Millie!

MILLIE
(calling)
But your cake!

ALICE-MIRANDA
(calling)
Do it!

So MILLIE shoves the trolley towards PETER . . .

. . . but PETER leaps out of the way and runs off, while the trolley <THUDS> into the wall, making the beautiful cake slide off and <SPLAT> onto the floor.

MILLIE/JACINTA/LUCAS
No!

ALICE-MIRANDA has caught up to MILLIE.

ALICE-MIRANDA
(calling)
It's just a cake!

The gang are closing in on PETER along a corridor when PETER, using the sceptre, pole-vaults over the railing and lands with a <THUMP> on the level below near a trolley of towels outside a door.

JACINTA climbs onto the railing and backflips over, down a level. LUCAS watches in amazement.

LUCAS
Cool!

JACINTA lands perfectly behind PETER in a crouch.

JACINTA
Gotcha!

But PETER kicks the towels off the trolley. They land in front of JACINTA, who leaps back to avoid them.

JACINTA (CONT'D)

Whoa!

PETER sprints off. The others hurry down the stairs, catch up to JACINTA and continue the chase.

Finally, PETER turns a corner. The kids follow but the corridor is empty.

MILLIE

Where's he gone?

There are identical doors all the way along the corridor. ALICE-MIRANDA zeroes in on one door which is slowly closing with a green flashing light next to it.

ALICE-MIRANDA

There!

She races over and grabs the handle just before it shuts. Then she puts her finger to her lips.

Cautiously, ALICE-MIRANDA eases the door open and peeks through.

SCENE 28: INT. CRUISE SHIP – DECK 2 – SEA LEVEL – NIGHT

This is the sea-level deck, with lifeboats; large, medium and small lifebuoys on the walls, each with a dangling rope; and an exit to the sea.

PETER is examining a lifeboat on the wall. He's carrying the loaded laundry bag with the sceptre now sticking out the top.

ALICE-MIRANDA pops her head through the door. She spots PETER and gestures to the others to get down!

MILLIE, JACINTA and LUCAS crawl in and conceal themselves behind lifeboats and life jackets. ALICE-MIRANDA slips in and hides behind a pillar.

Finally, PETER finds what he's looking for – a lever on the wall.

PETER

Aha!

He pulls the lever. He watches, smirking, as the boat is mechanically lowered into the water.

ALICE-MIRANDA scans the walls. CLOSE ON identical levers on the wall near where MILLIE is hiding. ALICE-MIRANDA silently points them out to MILLIE.

In the shadows, MILLIE nods. She kneels and pushes her lever up. PETER'S boat begins to mechanically rise.

Frowning, he yanks his lever down . . . the boat drops again. MILLIE pushes her lever up and the boat rises.

ALICE-MIRANDA gives MILLIE a thumbs-up from her hiding spot.

PETER (CONT'D)

Gah!

Frustrated, PETER sets down the laundry bag with the sceptre sticking out the top, and yanks his lever with both hands.

ALICE-MIRANDA zeroes in on the laundry bag.

She waves to JACINTA, who is nearest, and points to the bag. JACINTA nods, crawls out a metre and grabs the laundry bag.

JACINTA slides the bag to ALICE-MIRANDA behind the pillar, and is crawling back to her hiding spot when PETER turns and sees her foot.

PETER (CONT'D)

What?

He grabs JACINTA and hauls her out.

JACINTA

Hey!

Quickly, he grabs the smallest lifebuoy from the wall and shoves it over JACINTA'S head to her waist, so her arms are jammed by her sides.

JACINTA (CONT'D)

Hey!

She wriggles but she's trapped. She tries to waddle off, but PETER grabs the rope attached to the ring so JACINTA is caught like a fish on a line.

PETER glances around – the laundry bag is missing. He turns on JACINTA, looking as if he's going to explode.

PETER

Where's the bag, you little brat?

ALICE-MIRANDA steps out from behind the pillar with the bag.

PETER (CONT'D)

You again!

It's a standoff. ALICE-MIRANDA and PETER face each other.

ALICE-MIRANDA

Is this what you're looking for?
Because I've got a deal.

PETER

I'm not playing games here, Little
Miss Prim.

At this insult, ALICE-MIRANDA stays cool.

ALICE-MIRANDA

Neither am I. You give me Jacinta
and I'll give you your bag. The
adults will be here any second, so
I suggest you decide quickly.

Seeing no other choice, PETER holds out his hand for the bag. ALICE-MIRANDA steps out and, carefully, they switch. ALICE-MIRANDA takes the rope attached to the lifebuoy, while PETER takes the bag. The switch is made.

Then PETER jumps in the boat and zooms off over the dark water with the jewellery bag.

JACINTA

Thank you, Alice-Miranda!

ALICE-MIRANDA hugs JACINTA. LUCAS pops up and hurries over, followed by MILLIE.

LUCAS

Jacinta!

LUCAS tries to yank the lifebuoy over JACINTA'S head, but it's stuck.

MILLIE and ALICE-MIRANDA join LUCAS in tugging at the lifebuoy, and with a <POP>, JACINTA is free. She rubs her arms.

LUCAS (CONT'D)

Jacinta, you were so brave.

ALICE-MIRANDA

The bravest.

Distant footsteps, and the door is flung open. AUNTY GEE, her BODYGUARD, MARJORIE, CECELIA, HUGH and AMBROSIA rush in.

CECELIA

Alice-Miranda!

HUGH and CECELIA hug ALICE-MIRANDA, then CECELIA hugs MILLIE. They check the girls over.

CECELIA (CONT'D)

Aunty Gee's security guard realised
the crown jewels were gone . . .
and then we discovered you'd
disappeared!

ALICE-MIRANDA

We're perfectly fine, Mum. Jacinta was very brave.

AMBROSIA hurries over to JACINTA and hugs her tight.

AMBROSIA

Sweetheart!

In the hug, JACINTA'S eyes widen in surprise, then she smiles. At this point, ALICE-MIRANDA turns to AMBROSIA.

CLOSE ON AMBROSIA'S fingers. They are bare.

ALICE-MIRANDA

Mrs Headlington-Bear, I'm so sorry your wedding ring was stolen too.

AMBROSIA flushes.

AMBROSIA

Ah, was it?

(insincere)

Oh dear . . .

As AMBROSIA turns back to JACINTA, AUNTY GEE hurries over to ALICE-MIRANDA.

AUNTY GEE

I'm so glad you're all safe.

ALICE-MIRANDA

Unfortunately, the thief got away with the crown jewels and everyone else's things. Except . . .

She ducks behind the pillar and pulls out the RUBY TIARA which sparkles in the shadowy room.

EVERYONE

(gasping)

MARJORIE

How . . .?

ALICE-MIRANDA

I took it when Jacinta slid me the bag. I thought if I took out

anything else, the thief might
notice.

Everyone breaks into applause and cheers. ALICE-MIRANDA blushes.

DISSOLVE TO:

SCENE 29: INT. CRUISE SHIP – CABIN/ OCEAN – CONTINUOUS – LATE NIGHT

ALICE-MIRANDA is in bed in her pyjamas with her teddy bear, Brummel.

ALICE-MIRANDA
I'm sad we didn't catch the thief,
Brummel, and my birthday cake
was ruined. But at least it was for a
good reason.

She sets Brummel down on the pillow beside her and continues to talk to him.

ALICE-MIRANDA (CONT'D)
And my birthday certainly was
exciting.

JACINTA and MILLIE burst in wearing pyjamas, carrying a plate holding a cupcake with a single candle on it.

JACINTA/MILLIE

(singing)

Happy birthday to you, happy
birthday to you . . .

ALICE-MIRANDA is overwhelmed. She blows out the candle.

ALICE-MIRANDA

You two are the best!

MILLIE

Come on, Alice-Miranda, you can
finally open your presents!

The girls shriek and giggle as ALICE-MIRANDA leaps off the bed and starts ripping open her presents.

We MOVE OUT through the balcony onto the dark ocean.

An orange shape can be seen, illuminated by the lights of the ship. We drift over the water towards it. It turns out to be the lifeboat the thief took, drifting in the dark water.

There's no one in it.

But as we push in CLOSE ON the boat, and peer inside, we see the porter's outfit abandoned on the floor . . .

Slowly, we PULL OUT from the lifeboat and the lit cruise ship as it glows in the night.

DISSOLVE TO:

ACT
2

SCENE 30: EXT. WINCHESTERFIELD-DOWNSFORDVALE GARDENS – DAY

Across Winchesterfield-Downsfordvale school, it's high spring! CHARLIE's seedlings burst into blossoms.

One delicate blossom detaches in the wind and drifts in the breeze past . . .
– Birds trilling in the trees.
– Mrs Smith setting out pies to cool in the kitchen.

The blossom floats and dances towards BONAPARTE, CHOPS and STUMPS, who are grazing in the grass. BONAPARTE lifts his head and snaps the blossom in his teeth as it passes.

BONAPARTE chews and swallows.

BONAPARTE

Delicious! I just love spring!

SCENE 31: EXT. WINCHESTERFIELD-DOWNSFORDVALE – HALL – DAY

ALICE-MIRANDA, MILLIE and JACINTA sit together at assembly.

MILLIE

(sighing)

Best holiday ever. And after the thief got away, Lucas was so worried about you for the rest of the trip.

MILLIE nudges JACINTA.

JACINTA

He was worried about all of us.

ALICE-MIRANDA twinkles.

ALICE-MIRANDA

You most of all.

JACINTA blushes. As MILLIE and ALICE-MIRANDA exchange an amused smile, MISS GRIMM steps up to the microphone.

MISS GRIMM

Welcome back, girls. First off, we will announce our new vice prefect. Our head prefect, Alethea Goldsworthy, will share the results of your vote last term.

ALETHEA flounces onstage and takes the microphone.

ALETHEA

As you all know, I've been head prefect for a while now and frankly, it's all work, work, work.

MILLIE leans over to ALICE-MIRANDA and JACINTA.

MILLIE

(whispering)

The only work she does is straightening her hair.

ALICE-MIRANDA and JACINTA muffle giggles.

ALETHEA

Anyway, I'm in charge of this school and since I'm so busy –

MISS GRIMM frowns.

MISS GRIMM

Alethea, please get to the point.

ALETHEA rolls her eyes.

ALETHEA

Alright, alright. Well, I need an assistant and you all know who the right person is.

ALETHEA winks at DANIKA in the front row. A confident DANIKA winks back. MISS GRIMM hands ALETHEA a piece of paper.

ALETHEA (CONT'D)

And my lucky assistant is . . .

ALETHEA'S face twists in disgust.

ALETHEA (CONT'D)

. . . Ashima? You're kidding!

STUDENTS

(cheering)

ASHIMA walks onstage and MISS GRIMM hands her a clipboard. An astonished ASHIMA leans into the microphone.

ASHIMA

Really? Wow! Thank you!

Everyone cheers. From the crowd, ALICE-MIRANDA gives a glowing ASHIMA a thumbs up.

MILLIE

I bet you had something to do with this, Alice-Miranda.

ALICE-MIRANDA shrugs.

ALICE-MIRANDA

No harm in letting everyone know who's the best person for the job.

Ashima is calm, reliable and
organised.

JACINTA and MILLIE giggle.

MISS GRIMM
It's going to be a busy few weeks.
We're getting ready for the
Winchesterfield Spring Fair,
where the Queen's Grand Prix
horse event will be held.

GIRLS
(excited murmur)

MISS GRIMM
Now, I'd like to introduce our
newest student. Please make
Caprice Radford welcome.
She will be sharing Jacinta
Headlington-Bear's room.

Everyone claps politely. JACINTA rolls her eyes.

JACINTA
Why do I always get the new girls
in my room?

CAPRICE steps onstage and looks around sourly. It's clear she doesn't think much of the other students.

ALICE-MIRANDA
(whispering)
Because you aren't sharing with anyone?

JACINTA
(grimacing)
Oh, whatever.

MISS GRIMM
Now, off to class, girls!

The girls disband. ALICE-MIRANDA and her friends walk off together.

ALICE-MIRANDA
We should make sure Caprice feels welcome at our midnight feast. I think once you spend some time together, you and Caprice will get on famously.

JACINTA huffs.

JACINTA

Ugh, Alice-Miranda, you're too nice!

SCENE 32: INT. WINCHESTERFIELD-DOWNSFORDVALE – ALICE-MIRANDA'S ROOM – NIGHT

SUSANNAH, IVORY, ASHIMA, MILLIE, JACINTA and ALICE-MIRANDA are crammed on the floor around a heaped basket of treats.

IVORY/SUSANNAH

Congratulations, Ashima!/We knew you could do it!

JACINTA

How about Alethea's face?

MILLIE

She looked like she was sucking on sour lollies.

The girls giggle.

ASHIMA

I have you to thank, Alice-Miranda. I never would have had the guts to try for vice prefect if you hadn't encouraged me.

MILLIE

It's great, so long as you don't dob us in for this feast, Ashima.

MILLIE gestures to the basket. ASHIMA takes a toffee and chews.

ASHIMA

(full mouth)

No way, I'd be in trouble too.

At this moment, the door is flung open and CAPRICE swans in. She lies on her bed and starts flicking through a magazine, looking bored.

ALICE-MIRANDA

Welcome to our midnight feast, Caprice.

CAPRICE looks up from her magazine without cracking a smile.

CAPRICE
What kind of lame midnight feast starts at nine pm?

The others look at each other, slightly annoyed. ALICE-MIRANDA doesn't mind.

ALICE-MIRANDA
(giggling)
Nine pm is the school tradition.

The other girls nod. Exactly!

ALICE-MIRANDA (CONT'D)
Caprice, would you like one of Granny Valentina's toffees?

CAPRICE gets up, takes a toffee and bites. She grimaces.

CAPRICE
That's the worst toffee I've ever tasted. I should know, because my mum's a famous celebrity chef.

MILLIE looks grim, and JACINTA nudges ALICE-MIRANDA.

JACINTA
(quietly)
I told you so.

ALICE-MIRANDA'S brow furrows. She's battered but not beaten by CAPRICE'S bad attitude. She turns to the group.

ALICE-MIRANDA
So is everyone excited about the Queen's Grand Prix and the fair? There are so many things we can enter.

JACINTA
I'm going to enter the cake competition.

ALICE-MIRANDA
That's great! Are you entering anything, Ivory?

IVORY shakes her head nervously.

IVORY

I was thinking about the pony events but I'm not sure about jumping.

ALICE-MIRANDA considers.

ALICE-MIRANDA

How about the pairs barrel racing? There's no jumping and it's lots of fun. Susannah wanted to try it.

SUSANNAH nods.

ALICE-MIRANDA (CONT'D)

Perhaps you could team up?

SUSANNAH

Yes! Please, Ivory?

IVORY looks nervous.

IVORY

But . . . I've never done barrel racing before.

ALICE-MIRANDA

Bony and I will help you train.

CAPRICE looks around the room.

CAPRICE

Who's Bony?

MILLIE

He's Alice-Miranda's pony, and he's quite a handful.

CAPRICE flips her hair.

CAPRICE

What kind of wimp can't manage a pony?

The girls look at each other . . .

ALICE-MIRANDA/MILLIE/IVORY/SUSANNAH

(laughing)

CAPRICE frowns. She doesn't like being laughed at.

CAPRICE

What's so funny?

JACINTA

You haven't met Bony.

ALICE-MIRANDA sees CAPRICE'S sour expression and, again, tries to save the situation.

ALICE-MIRANDA

The horse I can't wait to meet is Popstar! She's the Queen's prize mare and she'll be stabled right here at school.

IVORY

What kind of riding does the Queen do?

ALICE-MIRANDA

Popstar's a dressage mare, it's like horse-dancing. The horses do steps and pirouettes to music.

CAPRICE is still stung from being laughed at.

CAPRICE

Who'd want to meet the Queen's stupid horse? Mum's cooked for Queen Georgiana and she's full of herself. Her horse probably is too.

JACINTA leaps up, truly annoyed, and scowls at CAPRICE.

JACINTA

You mean Aunty Gee? She's super nice!

CAPRICE leaps up and scowls back at JACINTA.

CAPRICE

You're an expert on the Queen, are you?

MILLIE

(quietly to ALICE-MIRANDA)

They're getting on famously alright. Famous like the Titanic!

ALICE-MIRANDA winces. Right then, ALETHEA and the MARIONETTES bust in with water balloons.

ALETHEA

Get them!

After last time, the girls are prepared. ALICE-MIRANDA crouches and reaches deep into the treat basket.

ALICE-MIRANDA

Now!

ALICE-MIRANDA pulls out a foam water squirter. The other girls reach under pillows, and pull out more water squirters and soak the MARIONETTES back.

Splashing and shrieking ensue. JACINTA aims at ALETHEA, who ducks. The water splashes in a stream on CAPRICE'S chest.

CAPRICE

Argh!

A soaked CAPRICE glowers at JACINTA, who's busy squirting SHELBY.

CAPRICE (CONT'D)

(to herself)

You'll pay for this, Jacinta Headlington-Bear.

DISSOLVE TO:

SCENE 33: EXT. WINCHESTERFIELD COUNTRYSIDE – MORNING

The woods are scattered with wildflowers and butterflies. Up ahead in a clearing is a tumbledown old barn. We hear galloping <HOOF BEATS>. ALICE-MIRANDA appears on BONAPARTE, racing at top speed.

ALICE-MIRANDA

(calling)

Faster, Bony, faster! We've got to get to the old barn first!

BONAPARTE

Yeah!

LUCAS appears behind her on SPORT.

SPORT
(whinnying)
We're catching up!

BONAPARTE
(whinnying)
You think?

BONAPARTE puts on a spurt of speed and ALICE-MIRANDA reaches the barn first. The children slow their ponies to a walk.

LUCAS
Great race.

ALICE-MIRANDA
Yes, and it's terrific preparation for the barrel racing competition.

BONAPARTE
Competition? We'll win that for sure!

LUCAS

Hey, my dad and your Aunt Charlotte are coming to the Grand Prix. It's so cool they're dating.

They smile at each other.

ALICE-MIRANDA

Do you realise if they got married, you and I would be cousins?

LUCAS boggles. He hadn't thought of it.

LUCAS

Wow, you're right!

He turns SPORT and trots back up the path a little.

LUCAS (CONT'D)

Race you back!

SPORT takes off.

Then BONAPARTE takes off with ALICE-MIRANDA not quite ready.

ALICE-MIRANDA
Argh, Bony, slow down!

DISSOLVE TO:

<u>SCENE 34: EXT. WINCHESTERFIELD-DOWNSFORDVALE STABLES – DAY</u>

As ALICE-MIRANDA trots in on BONAPARTE, she sees a float with the royal crest on it parked outside.

ALICE-MIRANDA
(to BONAPARTE)
I think Popstar's here.

ALICE-MIRANDA leaves BONAPARTE in the yard.

POPSTAR (O.S.)
(whinnying)

ALICE-MIRANDA hurries inside.

<u>SCENE 35: INT. WINCHESTERFIELD-DOWNSFORDVALE STABLES – DAY</u>

ALICE-MIRANDA enters the stables and looks around.

POPSTAR (O.S.)
(whinnying)

SAM (O.S.)
Popstar, come on!

ALICE-MIRANDA sees POPSTAR, an elegant, tall dressage mare, resisting being put into her stall by SAM, a female stablehand in a purple shirt.

POPSTAR won't go. SAM steps back.

ALICE-MIRANDA
Hello, I'm Alice-Miranda.

SAM nods at ALICE-MIRANDA as she's clutching POPSTAR'S reins in both hands.

SAM
I'm Sam, I've just started working
with Charlie . . . whoa, girl!

POPSTAR rears up. SAM struggles to control her.

POPSTAR

(snorting)

ALICE-MIRANDA

(to herself)

That looks dangerous.

(to SAM)

Do you need help?

POPSTAR tugs and shifts, rolling her eyes.

SAM

(struggling)

I can't wait until the new trainer arrives – maybe he can control her.

SAM tugs POPSTAR again but she won't move.

POPSTAR

Help!

BONAPARTE (O.S.)

(whinnying)

I'm coming!

POPSTAR freezes. Her ears are pricked up. She lifts her head.

POPSTAR

(whinnying)

Get me out of here!

BONAPARTE canters inside and rushes past ALICE-MIRANDA, towards POPSTAR. SAM drops POPSTAR'S reins and backs away in fright.

ALICE-MIRANDA is startled.

ALICE-MIRANDA

Bony?!

BONAPARTE passes ALICE-MIRANDA and goes straight up to POPSTAR. He reaches up and touches his nose to POPSTAR'S.

BONAPARTE

Relax, everything's A-okay.

POPSTAR quietens. Instant connection! SAM and ALICE-MIRANDA stare.

ALICE-MIRANDA
I think they just made friends.

And they have, standing there together quietly.

Then ALICE-MIRANDA has an idea. She turns, with a twinkling smile, to SAM.

ALICE-MIRANDA (CONT'D)
I think I know how to get Popstar into her stall.

ALICE-MIRANDA takes BONAPARTE'S reins and leads him into the stall next to POPSTAR.

BONAPARTE
(to POPSTAR)
C'mon, we can be neigh-bours.
Ha-ha!

By herself, POPSTAR steps into her stall, which is beside BONAPARTE'S. SAM <SLAMS> the door shut.

SAM
Amazing!

ALICE-MIRANDA

I think they're going to be best friends.

ALICE-MIRANDA gazes at the horse and pony standing with their noses touching over the barrier.

BONAPARTE

Too right.

SCENE 36: INT. WINCHESTERFIELD-DOWNSFORDVALE STABLES/GRANNY VALENTINA'S HOUSE – DAY

Still in riding gear, ALICE-MIRANDA dials the stable phone.

ALICE-MIRANDA

Hi, Granny, it's Alice-Miranda. May I speak to Aunty Gee?

START SPLIT SCREEN:

At the other end, AUNTY GEE presses a button and the call goes on speaker.

ALICE-MIRANDA (CONT'D)

Hi, Aunty Gee, I thought I'd let you know Popstar's arrived and Bony's calmed her down. When are you coming to see her?

AUNTY GEE looks around. We see the BODY-GUARD guarding the door, and MARJORIE on an armchair on her laptop.

GRANNY VALENTINA is sitting on the sofa beside AUNTY GEE, holding a tea cup.

AUNTY GEE

(sighing)

It's too dangerous. Our thief is still out there somewhere and the emails keep coming.

ALICE-MIRANDA

But you'll have to train on Popstar before the Grand Prix, surely.

AUNTY GEE looks at MARJORIE, who shakes her head.

AUNTY GEE

I don't think I'll be riding Popstar in the Grand Prix at all.

ALICE-MIRANDA is dismayed.

ALICE-MIRANDA

Aunty Gee, I'm sure we can find a way!

AUNTY GEE smiles ruefully.

AUNTY GEE

I know you're clever, my dear, but I think this might be too hard, even for you.

ALICE-MIRANDA isn't put off.

ALICE-MIRANDA

Trust me, Aunty Gee – I'll call you back when I think of something. Anyway don't worry about Popstar. Now she's with Bony, she's as gentle as a lamb.

ALICE-MIRANDA hangs up.

END SPLIT SCREEN

GRANNY VALENTINA'S HOUSE: AUNTY GEE puts down the phone, shakes her head.

AUNTY GEE

Poor Alice-Miranda will be disappointed when she realises I can't ride. Well, the new trainer will just have to manage Popstar without me. He has an excellent resume.

MARJORIE nods firmly. She's happy with AUNTY GEE staying under lock and key.

MARJORIE

Quite right, Your Majesty.

Frowning, AUNTY GEE turns to GRANNY VALENTINA.

AUNTY GEE

Val, am I doing the right thing?

I mean, how long should I hide away? Should I be hiding away at all?

GRANNY VALENTINA sips her tea thoughtfully.

GRANNY VALENTINA

People expect to see the Queen around the Queen's Grand Prix. I think it's worth the risk.

MARJORIE steps forward, frowning.

MARJORIE

Her Majesty must stay safe at all times. We can reassess your security closer to your Silver Jubilee celebrations later in the year.

AUNTY GEE

Oh, yes, I forgot about my Jubilee.

AUNTY GEE looks back and forth between GRANNY VALENTINA and MARJORIE, then slumps on the sofa, looking old and defeated. GRANNY VALENTINA puts an arm around her.

AUNTY GEE (CONT'D)

Val, I don't know what to do anymore. What kind of leader have I become?

SCENE 37: INT. WINCHESTERFIELD-DOWNSFORDVALE STABLES/YARD – DAY

Next morning, JACINTA and MILLIE are feeding and grooming BUTTERCUP and CHOPS in their stalls. CAPRICE stalks past them in riding gear. She doesn't notice MILLIE or JACINTA.

CAPRICE marches to BONAPARTE'S stall, where BONAPARTE and POPSTAR stand together. SAM, the stablehand, is sweeping.

MILLIE and JACINTA look at each other, surprised.

MILLIE

What's she up to?

CAPRICE

I'm going to ride that pony.

She points to BONAPARTE. The horses react.

BONAPARTE
Uh-oh . . .

SAM hesitates.

SAM
Isn't that Alice-Miranda's pony?

CAPRICE
She gave me permission.

MILLIE and JACINTA shrug.

JACINTA
Alice-Miranda is generous.

They watch as CAPRICE tries to take BONAPARTE from the stable. He stands like an immovable rock.

BONAPARTE
Nope, not going.

In the next stall POPSTAR goes mental, stamping and snorting.

POPSTAR

Hey, he stays with me!

SAM grabs POPSTAR'S bridle to hold her still.

SAM

Take him out quickly.

CAPRICE drags a resisting BONAPARTE out of his stall.

CAPRICE

Come on, you ridiculous pony!

BONAPARTE

Who are you?

Finally, she drags him out to the yard. MILLIE and JACINTA look at each other.

MILLIE

We can't miss this.

They follow.

SCENE 38: INT/EXT. WINCHESTERFIELD-DOWNSFORDVALE STABLES YARD – DAY

CAPRICE is in the yard about to mount the reluctant BONAPARTE.

CAPRICE
(muttering)
Think I can't manage a pony, do you?

As she's about to swing up, BONAPARTE steps away from her and she stumbles.

BONAPARTE
Not this one.

MILLIE and JACINTA poke their heads out the door, watching in disbelief.

Then BONAPARTE nips CAPRICE'S hair.

CAPRICE
Ow! You little –

BONAPARTE SHOVES her into a hedge with his bottom.

CAPRICE (CONT'D)

Argh!

JACINTA and MILLIE stare. BONAPARTE farts, then trots back into the stables to join POPSTAR.

BONAPARTE

Bye-bye.

CAPRICE heaves herself out of the hedge. She's covered in foliage and in a rage.

CAPRICE

Ugh!

She storms off.

MILLIE/JACINTA

(stifling giggles)

DISSOLVE TO:

SCENE 39: EXT. WINCHESTERFIELD-DOWNSFORDVALE EQUESTRIAN FIELD – DAY

ALICE-MIRANDA stands in the grass as SUSANNAH and IVORY set off together towards the barrels.

SUSANNAH'S pony starts racing, but IVORY'S horse hesitates, then stops and won't move.

IVORY

(to pony)

Come on!

(calling to ALICE-MIRANDA)

Ugh, she won't move.

ALICE-MIRANDA comes over to the frustrated IVORY.

ALICE-MIRANDA

Try to relax and soften your grip – I think you're blocking her.

Then SAM, the stablehand, comes to the fence.

SAM

(calling)

Alice-Miranda, you're wanted in Miss Grimm's office.

Waving, ALICE-MIRANDA sets off.

SCENE 40: EXT/INT. MISS GRIMM'S OFFICE – DAY

ALICE-MIRANDA arrives at MISS GRIMM'S office and taps on the door.

She opens it to find a bristling CAPRICE, in her dirty riding jacket, standing in front of MISS GRIMM'S desk. INKY the kitten is curled in the headmistress's lap, <PURRING>.

ALICE-MIRANDA enters. INKY leaps off MISS GRIMM'S lap and winds herself around ALICE-MIRANDA'S legs. ALICE-MIRANDA reaches down to pat her.

MISS GRIMM

Alice-Miranda, Caprice is making a formal complaint against Bony.

CAPRICE lifts her chin.

CAPRICE

Your pony's a dangerous animal who should be kicked out of the school!

ALICE-MIRANDA is stunned. She steps forward passionately.

ALICE-MIRANDA

Miss Grimm, Bony's naughty but he's not dangerous! What's he done?

At that remark, the door bursts open and MILLIE and JACINTA, in riding gear, tumble into the room.

MILLIE

(in a rush)

Please, Miss Grimm, Caprice was dragging Bony into the yard when he didn't want to go –

CAPRICE stamps.

CAPRICE

That's a lie!

JACINTA

No! That's why he nipped you!

You're the liar!

CAPRICE glares at MILLIE and JACINTA, who have clearly been eavesdropping through the door. MISS GRIMM blinks at this stream of information.

MISS GRIMM

I have an idea.

She presses a button and the secret entrance to her security room opens.

SCENE 41: INT. MISS GRIMM'S OFFICE – SECURITY ROOM – DAY

MISS GRIMM walks in, followed by the girls. CAPRICE stares in surprise at all the screens. MISS GRIMM plays with a few buttons.

A video of CAPRICE dragging BONAPARTE into the yard plays in fast motion. MISS GRIMM raises her eyebrows and turns to CAPRICE.

MISS GRIMM

It appears you did drag Bony into the yard when he was resisting.

CAPRICE blushes. MILLIE and JACINTA both glare at CAPRICE.

MILLIE

Did you even ask to ride Bony?

Everyone looks at a fuming, mortified CAPRICE. She's silent. ALICE-MIRANDA turns to CAPRICE.

ALICE-MIRANDA

She didn't, but she's welcome to ride Bony with my help. He just doesn't take well to strangers.

CAPRICE looks as if she's going to explode. Then ALICE-MIRANDA turns to MISS GRIMM, smiling.

ALICE-MIRANDA (CONT'D)
Miss Grimm, I thought you'd got rid of the cameras?

Now it's MISS GRIMM'S turn to blush.

MISS GRIMM
They're for security reasons. Off you go, girls.

MISS GRIMM (CONT'D)
Caprice, I trust you'll think hard before you throw around these sort of accusations again.

CAPRICE marches out of the office, fuming.

DISSOLVE TO:

SCENE 42: INT. WINCHESTERFIELD-DOWNSFORDVALE HALL – DAY

CAPRICE is on the hall phone.

ALICE-MIRANDA is standing further down the hall, waiting for the phone and happens to overhear.

CAPRICE (O.S.)
Thanks, Mummy, I knew you'd know what was going on. I promise I won't tell a soul.

ALICE-MIRANDA peers at CAPRICE, who hangs up, then looks around the hall with a devious expression.

CAPRICE spots ALETHEA, SHELBY and DANIKA down the hall and sprints off after them.

CAPRICE (CONT'D)
(calling)
Girls! Do I have some juicy goss for you!

ALICE-MIRANDA steps out and picks up the phone and dials.

ALICE-MIRANDA
Hi, Granny, may I speak to Aunty Gee for a moment? Aunty Gee, I've got an idea . . .

DISSOLVE TO:

SCENE 43: INT. WINCHESTERFIELD-DOWNSFORDVALE CORRIDOR – DAY

ALICE-MIRANDA is walking along the corridor, having hung up the phone, when ALETHEA stops in front of her.

ALETHEA

Hey, Alice-Miranda.

ALETHEA gestures for ALICE-MIRANDA to follow her into the corner.

ALETHEA (CONT'D)

(low voice)

Listen – it's not that I like her or anything, but I think you should know about a rumour I've just heard . . .

ALICE-MIRANDA'S face changes.

SCENE 44: INT. WINCHESTERFIELD-DOWNSFORDVALE DINING ROOM – DAY

Inside the dining room, JACINTA is eating lunch.

She hears whispering around her. She narrows her eyes and glances around.

A pair of girls behind her stop talking and look away. She looks to another table, and the same thing happens.

She looks down at her plate and the whispering starts again.

JACINTA is ruffled. ALICE-MIRANDA slips into the seat beside JACINTA, without lunch.

JACINTA

Alice-Miranda? I think everyone's talking about me.

ALICE-MIRANDA

(low voice)

Look, there's something you should know. It may not be true but it's what's being said.

JACINTA stiffens.

JACINTA

(low voice)

What is it?

CLOSE ON ALICE-MIRANDA, twirling her hair.

We FLASH BACK to AMBROSIA'S bare hands from scene twenty-seven, without wedding ring.

ALICE-MIRANDA leans close to JACINTA.

ALICE-MIRANDA

(low voice)

They're saying your parents are getting a divorce. I think you should try to call your mum.

JACINTA gapes at ALICE-MIRANDA, who sees JACINTA is in shock, so takes her hand.

ALICE-MIRANDA (CONT'D)

(low voice)

Let's get out of here.

Without fuss, ALICE-MIRANDA leads JACINTA out.

SCENE 45: INT. WINCHESTERFIELD-DOWNSFORDVALE CORRIDOR – DAY

ALICE-MIRANDA takes JACINTA to the same stretch of corridor where ALETHEA told her about the rumour. MILLIE arrives, having heard the chatter.

MILLIE
I hope it's not true, Jacinta.

JACINTA nods, tearing up. She wipes her face.

JACINTA
Me too, but who knows. Mum's been acting weirder than usual.

ALICE-MIRANDA puts her arm around JACINTA.

ALICE-MIRANDA
Whatever happens, we're here for you. Friends forever.

The three girls hug.

MILLIE/JACINTA
Friends forever.

TRANSITION TO:

SCENE 46: EXT. SCHOOL – EARLY MORNING

It's the first morning of the Winchesterfield Fair, bright and early. ALICE-MIRANDA and MILLIE are on their way to visit their ponies. ALICE-MIRANDA has a satchel full of treats.

Both girls are hop, skip and jumping excitedly.

MILLIE
I can't wait for the pairs barrel racing. We're going to be an awesome pair and so are Bony and Chops.

As they enter the stables, it's immediately clear that POPSTAR and BONAPARTE are still best of friends. They're in adjoining stalls leaning gently into each other. They don't even notice the girls come in.

ALICE-MIRANDA
Speaking of pairs, check that out.

MILLIE

So sweet. Lucky Bony wasn't expelled after Caprice's complaint.

ALICE-MIRANDA

Lucky for Bony and for Popstar.

TRANSITION TO:

SCENE 47: FRIENDSHIP – VARIOUS LOCATIONS – DAY

MONTAGE as we see BONAPARTE and POPSTAR:
– Grooming each other, making happy <SNORTS> and <NEIGHS>.
– Frolicking together on the grass outside the stable.
– POPSTAR in training with BONAPARTE watching nearby, ridden respectively by SAM and ALICE-MIRANDA.

POPSTAR performs a dressage move beautifully then eyes BONAPARTE, fluttering her long eyelashes.

POPSTAR

Impressed?

BONAPARTE <NEIGHS> in appreciation.

BONAPARTE

Sure am. How about this?

He tries to copy her move but backs into a tree. Oops! Both horses laugh.

BONAPARTE/POPSTAR

(whinnying)

TRANSITION TO:

SCENE 48: INT. SCHOOL STABLES – EARLY MORNING

The girls pause to watch the pair for a moment.

POPSTAR

(quietly to BONAPARTE)

I get so nervous before an event.

BONAPARTE

Here's what I do when I'm nervous . . .

He farts.

POPSTAR
(whinnying laugh)

ALICE-MIRANDA holds her nose. So does MILLIE.

ALICE-MIRANDA
Bony! Pee-ew!
(giggles)
Though Popstar doesn't seem to mind.

MILLIE
Well, I'm making a fast escape.
(calling)
Chops! Chops!

MILLIE leaves to visit CHOPS. ALICE-MIRANDA feeds BONAPARTE a carrot.

ALICE-MIRANDA
Here, Bony, your favourite.

POPSTAR sniffs ALICE-MIRANDA'S satchel.

ALICE-MIRANDA (CONT'D)

Don't worry, Popstar. I haven't forgotten your favourite . . .

She pulls some red cabbage from her satchel. We see a shadow fall over her. Someone's behind her.

ALICE-MIRANDA (CONT'D)

. . . red cabbage.

BONAPARTE and POPSTAR munch happily.

TOM (O.S.)

This must be the famous Popstar.

ALICE-MIRANDA'S startled and spins around quickly. It's POPSTAR'S new trainer, TOM. He notices POPSTAR enjoying the cabbage.

ALICE-MIRANDA

Oh, hello, you must be Popstar's new trainer. I'm Alice-Miranda.

She extends her hand. He shakes it firmly.

TOM

Stand aside, young lady – I'll take it from here.

As TOM flings open POPSTAR'S stall door, the horse gets tetchy. Her ears pin back, her tail swishes violently, she purses her lips and <WHINNIES> anxiously.

POPSTAR

No you won't!

But the trainer doesn't read the warning signs. He steps closer to grab her bridle and she rears up.

POPSTAR (CONT'D)

(whinnying)

He steps back, perplexed.

TOM

She does seem upset by something. Now, come on, girl, we've got a job to do.

ALICE-MIRANDA pipes up.

ALICE-MIRANDA

Why not take Bony out with Popstar? They go everywhere together.

TOM leans on POPSTAR'S stall door.

TOM

That won't be necessary. In fact, what Popstar needs is less distractions. So run along and leave us to it . . .

ALICE-MIRANDA

Oh. Alright.

ALICE-MIRANDA leaves, a little hurt by the trainer's abrupt manner.

SCENE 49: EXT. WINCHESTERFIELD FAIR – ESTABLISHING SHOT – DAY

By mid-morning the small country fair is in full swing. Barrels have been set up on the equestrian field. There are colourful marquees and bunting.

Three stalls sit in a row on the periphery: the wackiest vegetable stall, the funniest flower arrangement stall and the fanciest cake stall. There's a small podium with a microphone and stand nearby.

ALETHEA (O.S.)
Roll on up. Or whatever they say.

SCENE 50: EXT. WINCHESTERFIELD FAIR – PODIUM/VEGETABLE STALL – DAY

SMALL PODIUM: ASHIMA struggles to carry a stack of wrapped prizes with a fancy hat balanced on top, while ALETHEA wears a headset microphone and flips her hair.

ALETHEA
Time for the Alethea Goldsworthy
raffle to be drawn. All profits go to
the Alethea Goldsworthy Library.
That's me, Alethea Goldsworthy.
Assistant, pass me the first ticket.

ASHIMA struggles to balance the prizes in one arm while pulling a ticket stub from the fancy hat on top.

ALETHEA (CONT'D)

Yawn. Any time you're ready.

ASHIMA hands the ticket to ALETHEA, almost dropping the prize stack as she does.

ALETHEA (CONT'D)

We have our first winner. Ticket Blue 21.

BOY

Me. Me!

He rushes forwards and grabs a prize from the bottom of the stack ASHIMA is holding.

ASHIMA

No!

The hat and the prizes <CRASH> to the ground, sending raffle tickets fluttering everywhere. ASHIMA drops to her knees and starts scooping them up.

ALETHEA raises an eyebrow, making no move to help. One raffle ticket flutters down in front of her face and she catches it.

ALETHEA

Must I do everything myself?

WACKIEST VEGETABLE STALL: ALICE-MIRANDA, MILLIE and JACINTA (in riding gear) are laughing at the array of funny vegetables. There are some hilarious twisted carrots, tomatoes and peppers.

ALICE-MIRANDA/MILLIE/JACINTA

(laughing)

Look!/Check that one out!/Crazy!

CECELIA approaches holding an ice cream.

CECELIA

Darling, hello!

ALICE-MIRANDA hugs her mum.

ALICE-MIRANDA

(quietly)

Is Aunty Gee coming?

CECELIA

(whispering)

Still under tight security, I'm afraid.

MILLIE

But she'll be missed at the Grand Prix tomorrow.

CECELIA

Yes . . .

(sadly)

. . . people love to see their Queen.

Their attention is drawn by laughter nearby. It's the PRINCES shaking up cans of soda and spraying them at each other.

PRINCE EDGAR/PRINCE LOUIS

(laughing and screaming)

The PRINCES turn, almost spraying ALICE-MIRANDA and MILLIE, who leap back.

PRINCE EDGAR

Whoops, sorry, Alice-Miranda!

MILLIE turns to ALICE-MIRANDA in astonishment.

MILLIE

Since when were the princes your
friends?

ALICE-MIRANDA shrugs.

ALICE-MIRANDA

They've been nice to me since
I stuck up for them on the ship.

The PRINCES have also caught ALETHEA'S eye as she stands above ASHIMA, who is on her knees gathering the fallen raffle tickets. The prizes lie on the ground.

ALETHEA

They must be the twin princes –
I saw them in *Goss and Gloss*. The
oldest one will be King one day!
I wonder which one he is.

She waves and flicks her hair flirtatiously. They don't glance over.

ASHIMA

They're going to Fayle School, so we'll be seeing a lot more of them.

ALETHEA raises her eyebrows.

ALETHEA

Don't get any ideas, Ashima. As head prefect, I get first pick.

There's a P.A. <CRACKLE> followed by an announcement.

P.A. SYSTEM (O.S.)

Calling all contestants in the junior barrel racing.

ASHIMA

Got to go. Sorry.

She stuffs the raffle tickets into the hat. Nearby MILLIE, JACINTA and ALICE-MIRANDA squeal with excitement.

CECELIA

(calling)

Best of luck, girls!

TRANSITION TO:

SCENE 51: EXT. WINCHESTERFIELD EQUESTRIAN FIELD – SOON AFTER

Under a modest pavilion, a crowd is watching the riders on their ponies about to start the races. The crowd includes LUCAS, AMBROSIA, AUNT CHARLOTTE, LAWRENCE, CECELIA AND GRANNY VALENTINA. POPSTAR is tied up outside the fence.

MISS HIGGINS ON P.A. SYSTEM (O.S.)

Presenting pair number one:
Susannah and Ivory.

CLOSE ON the two girls, mounted.

SUSANNAH

Ready partner?

IVORY

Not really . . .

MISS HIGGINS ON P.A. SYSTEM (O.S.)

Three . . . two . . . one . . . go!

They squeal and off they race, in perfect sync, around one barrel, then another, then a third in a clover pattern. They grab flags from the barrels as they go, before crossing a finishing line. The crowd <APPLAUDS>. SUSANNAH and IVORY laugh with joy and relief.

MISS HIGGINS ON P.A. SYSTEM (O.S.)

(enthusiastic)

Tremendous effort girls. And your ponies. Now we have Alice-Miranda and Millie. Three . . . two . . . one . . . go!

CLOSE ON the girls. BONAPARTE lets loose a loud fart! ALICE-MIRANDA grimaces.

ALICE-MIRANDA

Bony!

But the race has begun and she speeds to catch up to MILLIE on CHOPS. They gather their flags and cross the finish line.

More <APPLAUSE> from the small but enthusiastic crowd.

BONAPARTE
(to POPSTAR)
Bony the Pony goes for gold!

POPSTAR
(giggling)

MISS HIGGINS ON P.A. SYSTEM (O.S.)
Finally, Jacinta and Ashima.

They also put on a crowd-pleasing performance. AMBROSIA, in the crowd, loudly cheers her daughter along.

AMBROSIA
Go Jacinta! Go, go –

Then AMBROSIA'S <RINGTONE> sounds. She stops cheering to take a call on her mobile.

Horses and riders gather to hear the results. The crowd hushes.

MISS HIGGINS ON P.A. SYSTEM (O.S.)

And, by a whisker . . . the gold goes to . . .

(pause)

Susannah and Ivory!

ALICE-MIRANDA

Hooray!

The crowd and the girls go wild. ALICE-MIRANDA turns to MILLIE and JACINTA.

ALICE-MIRANDA (CONT'D)

They worked so hard. They deserve to win.

JACINTA'S distracted, seeing her mother in the crowd.

JACINTA

Mum!

She quickly dismounts and hands BUTTERCUP'S reins to ASHIMA. The girls and ponies leave the arena.

JACINTA rushes up to her mum, who is still on the phone.

JACINTA (CONT'D)

Mum. Mum! Your wedding ring wasn't stolen was it?!

AMBROSIA

Darling, I'm on the phone!

JACINTA

You're always on the phone. Why can't you ever make time for me?!

AMBROSIA

(startled)

Oh, sorry. Err, I'll call you back.

AMBROSIA hangs up her phone. She looks at her angry daughter.

JACINTA

You and Daddy are getting a divorce. Admit it.

AMBROSIA slowly nods.

AMBROSIA

So you know.

JACINTA

(furious)

Of course I know! If only you'd told me before the whole school knew, wouldn't it have been better?

AMBROSIA

But . . . how did . . .? Yes, darling . . . you should have been the first to know. It's just that I – I –

AMBROSIA is about to say something when her <RINGTONE> sounds again. She looks at JACINTA, teary, then at the number on the screen.

AMBROSIA (CONT'D)
Sorry, honey, but I really have to take this one.

She claps the phone to her ear and JACINTA turns on her heel and storms off.

MISS HIGGINS ON P.A. SYSTEM (O.S.)
Judging is about to begin at the stalls. Hurry on over, folks.

The crowd leaves but AMBROSIA remains, still on her phone.

SCENE 52: EXT. BEHIND A MARQUEE – SHORT CUT – SOON AFTER

ALICE-MIRANDA and MILLIE are running to the stalls via a short cut between the marquees.

MILLIE
(puffing)
I promise this is a short cut!

They turn a corner past SAM, the stablehand, in close discussion with TOM, POPSTAR'S new trainer.

ALICE-MIRANDA
Isn't that Sam and the new trainer?

SAM and TOM turn, startled to see the girls. They all stare for a beat, then the girls hurry on.

TOM
That girl's everywhere!

SCENE 53: EXT. WHACKIEST VEGETABLE STALL – SOON AFTER

The girls join the crowd at the stall. The wackiest vegetable is being judged by MISS GRIMM. She chooses a carrot shaped like a foot.

MISS GRIMM
I'm pleased to announce the
winner of the wackiest vegetable
is this cute little carrot, or should
I say foot?

The crowd laughs.

MISS GRIMM (CONT'D)
And next, the funniest flower
arrangement.

Alice-Miranda, Caprice, Millie, Jacinta, Ashima, Susannah, Ivory and Alethea

Marjorie, Lord Lloyd Lancaster-Brown, Granny Valentina, Queen Georgiana, Alice-Miranda, Millie, Lucas, Jacinta, Prince Edgar and Prince Louis

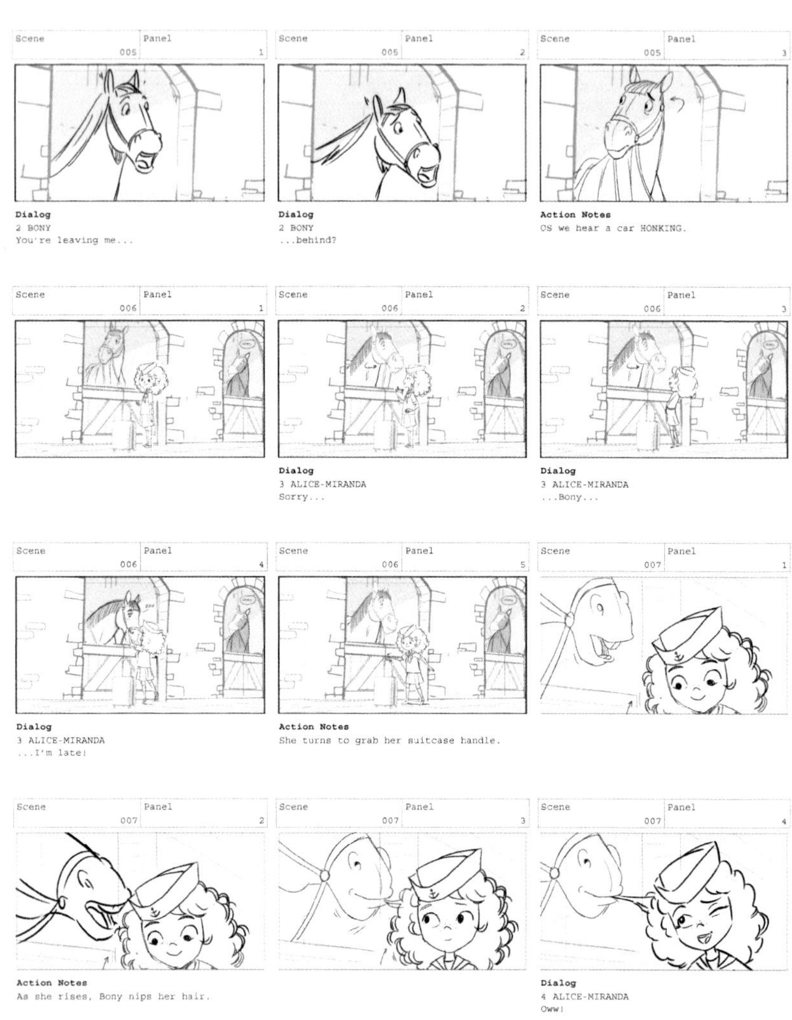

The process of animation starts with storyboarding.

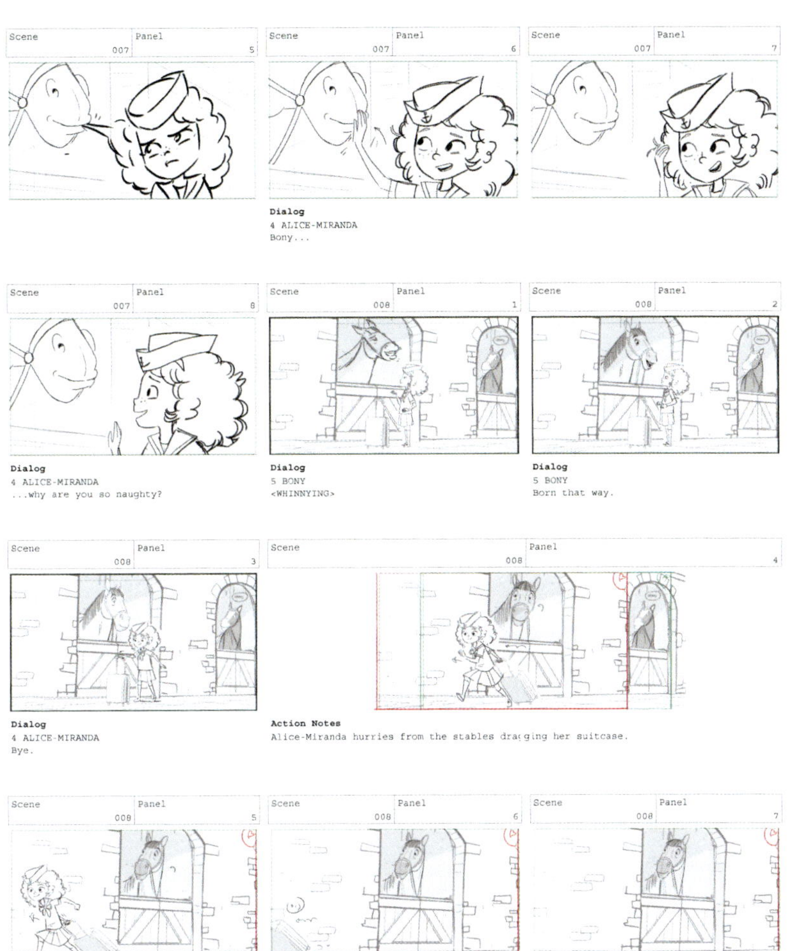

The entire movie is sketched out.

Artists refine storyboard sketches to create a layout . . .

. . . and then the final art!

Inside *The Queen Georgiana* . . .

The library

The dining room

The girls' room

The Winchesterfield Spring Fair . . .

The fanciest cake stall

The funniest flower arrangement stall

The wackiest vegetable stall

The Royal Christmas Ball . . .

Winchesterfield-Downsfordvale

Party time!

SCENE 54: EXT. FUNNIEST FLOWER ARRANGEMENT STALL – CONTINUOUS

She steps across to the adjoining stall, where CHARLIE is in attendance.

MISS GRIMM

Hello, Charlie, I see there are some great entries this year!

CHARLIE smiles. As MISS GRIMM looks closely at the flower arrangements, we focus on two flower sculptures of human heads with flowers for hair. ANGLE ON the heads.

MISS GRIMM (CONT'D)

These are very original.

The PRINCES have outdone themselves, making their heads into flower sculptures. Their faces are in white make-up.

MISS GRIMM (CONT'D)

In fact, I declare these very life-like statues the winners!

When they are judged as winners, the PRINCES burst into to life, leaping up.

PRINCE EDGAR/PRINCE LOUIS

Hooray!/Woo hoo!

Everyone's startled.

CROWD

Eek!/They're alive!/Oh my gosh!

The PRINCES brush off their flower disguises and bow. There's laughter and <APPLAUSE> from the crowd.

MISS GRIMM

That was unexpected. Are living sculptures allowed?

ALICE-MIRANDA is distracted. She's looking towards JACINTA.

MILLIE

Alice-Miranda is something wrong?

ALICE-MIRANDA

I just hope Jacinta's okay.

<u>SCENE 55: EXT. FANCIEST CAKE STALL – CONTINUOUS</u>

At the third stall, where MISS HIGGINS is supervising, CAPRICE proudly arrives carrying her croquembouche, and places it on a small table next to the main table. Beside it, on the main table, is JACINTA'S own entry – a lovely layered cake.

It's clearly smaller than CAPRICE'S.

MISS HIGGINS

Ooh! That's spectacular, Caprice.
Let's find a special spot for it. Yes.
Next to Jacinta's lovely cake!

JACINTA is looking off sadly towards her Mum who is on her phone again, CAPRICE notices.

CAPRICE

No way! It should go front of
Jacinta's.

CAPRICE notices JACINTA and grins sarcastically.

CAPRICE (CONT'D)
Hi, Jacinta, were you the last to hear about your parents' divorce? Wow, you'd think they'd tell you first. Guess they forgot about you.

It's really mean and JACINTA is infuriated.

JACINTA
(gritting teeth)
Life's full of disappointments, isn't it?

CAPRICE turns away.

JACINTA takes that moment to nudge the leg of the small table. CAPRICE'S croquembouche wobbles –

CAPRICE
No!

– then topples off the table and crashes to the ground.

CROWD
(gasping)

MISS HIGGINS rushes over. She and CAPRICE crouch and try to pick up the pieces of the ruined croquembouche.

MISS HIGGINS

And it was so lovely.

JACINTA quickly slips into the CROWD. Everyone saw the croquembouche fall but nobody, not even CAPRICE, saw JACINTA knock the table.

CAPRICE (O.S.)

That took me hours!

TRANSITION TO:

SCENE 56: EXT. WINCHESTERFIELD HOUSE – SUNSET

The sun sets over Winchesterfield House as the lights flicker off one by one, guided by the weary tones of MRS HOWARD, the house mistress.

MRS HOWARD (O.S.)

Lights out, girls!

It's an early night for everyone.

ALICE-MIRANDA/MILLIE (O.S.)
Good night, Howie.

Another light (theirs) flickers off.

SCENE 57: INT. WINCHESTERFIELD HOUSE – ALICE-MIRANDA AND MILLIE'S DORM – NIGHT

Illuminated by the moonlight, the girls, in pyjamas, pull up their covers.

MILLIE
(yawning)
Officially exhausted. Wake me next week.

ALICE-MIRANDA
I officially second that.

They settle down. ALICE-MIRANDA becomes reflective.

ALICE-MIRANDA (CONT'D)
I hope Jacinta will be okay. I'd be devastated if my parents got divorced.

MILLIE
Me too. Let's remember to be extra nice to her.
(yawning)

She turns over in bed. Another thought.

MILLIE (CONT'D)
Speaking of devastated. I'm upset that Aunty Gee can't ride Popstar
(yawning)
tomorrow.
(trailing off)

ALICE-MIRANDA notices that MILLIE is sound asleep . . . and smiles to herself.

ALICE-MIRANDA
True, but life's full of happy surprises, isn't it?

Her eyelids close and she also falls asleep. Only their breathing is heard.

NIGHT TO DAY TRANSITION:

SCENE 58: INT. WINCHESTERFIELD HOUSE – ALICE-MIRANDA AND MILLIE'S DORM – DAWN

At dawn we hear loud <NEIGHING> accompanied by <CRASHING> and <BANGING>. POPSTAR'S going berserk.

ALICE-MIRANDA wakes suddenly and sits up.

ALICE-MIRANDA

Popstar?!

She runs to the window and peers out but it's too dark to see much. She shakes MILLIE.

ALICE-MIRANDA (CONT'D)

Millie, wake up. Something's wrong at the stables.

SCENE 59: INT./EXT. SCHOOL STABLES – SOON AFTER

The girls sprint to the stables (after hastily throwing dressing gowns over their pyjamas) to find that BONAPARTE is missing.

His stable door is swinging open and the stall is empty! ALICE-MIRANDA is pale and worried.

ALICE-MIRANDA

Bony's gone!

POPSTAR'S bereft, <NEIGHING>, rearing and kicking the door to her stall. ALICE-MIRANDA looks around for clues.

ALICE-MIRANDA (CONT'D)

There must be an explanation.

MILLIE

Could he have run away?

She frowns at the open stable door.

ALICE-MIRANDA

No . . . I'm sure I latched his stall last night.

She looks down to see a small piece of torn purple cloth on the ground, as well as a chunk of red cabbage.

ALICE-MIRANDA (CONT'D)

Hmm . . .

CLOSE ON her face with eyes closed as we FLASHBACK to:

– SAM wearing the purple shirt.

– SAM in quiet conversation with TOM.

–ALICE-MIRANDA feeding POPSTAR red cabbage.

ALICE-MIRANDA opens her eyes and winds a strand of hair around her finger, deep in thought.

ALICE-MIRANDA (CONT'D)

Curious.

CLOSE ON an empty saddle hook.

ALICE-MIRANDA (CONT'D)

Look, his saddle's gone! Bony's clever, but he can't saddle himself.

MILLIE stares at the saddle hook.

MILLIE

You mean?

ALICE-MIRANDA

He's been horse-napped. And –

ALICE-MIRANDA holds out the piece of purple cloth . . .

ALICE-MIRANDA (CONT'D)

I think I know who took him.

MILLIE

Not Caprice!

ALICE-MIRANDA shakes her head.

ALICE-MIRANDA

No. Sam.

MILLIE isn't convinced.

MILLIE
Why would she steal Bony?

ALICE-MIRANDA
I don't know, but we need to find him. Maybe we can see which way they went.

They rush outside. ANGLE ON the dusty ground. There are some fresh hoof prints leading out into the woods. She points.

ALICE-MIRANDA (CONT'D)
Look! They couldn't have gone far.

MILLIE
Especially without Bony's cooperation.
(beat)
Let's get Chops.

They rush back into the stable and in an instant emerge on CHOPS, in their riding hats and boots.

As they follow the hoof prints they find they get muddled with dozens of other hoof prints.

ALICE-MIRANDA
There are too many prints from the other horses. Where would anyone hide a pony around here?

The girls share a concerned look. MILLIE shrugs. Together, they plunge into the dark woods.

DISSOLVE TO:

SCENE 60: EXT. WINCHESTERFIELD EQUESTRIAN FIELD – AN HOUR OR SO LATER

It's almost time for the Queen's Grand Prix equestrian events, and a stablehand is trying to coax POPSTAR from her stall.

She is nervy and twitchy, resisting.

STABLEHAND
(soothing)
Come on now, pet. Don't know

where your trainer is, but I've got you.

POPSTAR
(whinnying)
Not without Bony. Are you kidding?

SCENE 61: EXT. WOODS/DARK WOODS WITH OLD BARN – MEANWHILE

The girls are dirty, dishevelled and worried as they ride between leafy branches. They've been riding for ages. They check the time.

ALICE-MIRANDA
Almost noon. Popstar's event's in half an hour.

MILLIE
Where can Bony be? We need him.

CHOPS stumbles.

ALICE-MIRANDA
Chops! Are you okay?

He limps on.

MILLIE

He seems lame. Could it have been the barrel racing yesterday?

ALICE-MIRANDA

Or this long search . . .

The girls look at each other, alarmed by this development. They both dismount.

ALICE-MIRANDA (CONT'D)

(firmly)

You need to take him home to rest.

MILLIE

I know.

(torn)

But . . . Bony?!

ALICE-MIRANDA lifts her chin.

ALICE-MIRANDA

I'll find him. There's an old barn

near here that Lucas and I rode
past. It's worth a look.

She indicates a very dark part of the woods.

MILLIE

Are you sure you'll be okay alone?

ALICE-MIRANDA nods.

ALICE-MIRANDA

Yes, go look after Chops.

MILLIE leads a limping CHOPS towards home. ALICE-MIRANDA looks into the dark woods, and steps courageously towards them. Shards of sunlight shine down, breaking up the darkness.

ALICE-MIRANDA (CONT'D)

(to herself)

I'll find you, Bony. Dark woods
are just the same as the rest of the
woods, only with more trees.

A bird sounds an eerie <CALL>. ALICE-MIRANDA hesitates, then presses on.

She sees the rotten barn. It does look scary. CLOSE ON two sets of footprints and one set of hoof prints leading to it.

ALICE-MIRANDA'S face changes. Carefully, in silence, she creeps up to the barn.

ALICE-MIRANDA (CONT'D)
(scared breathing)

She hears a frightened <WHINNY>.

ALICE-MIRANDA (CONT'D)
(whispering)
Bony?

She places her ear to the old barn door and listens.

TOM (O.S.)
(yelling)
I said Popstar, you fool. Not this cranky useless animal!

ALICE-MIRANDA peers through a crack.

TOM and SAM are arguing right on the other side of the door. And behind them BONAPARTE is tied up.

TOM (CONT'D)
What did I pay you for, girl?

SAM bristles – she's sick of being yelled at.

SAM
What's the difference? Popstar was going so crazy she ripped my shirt. She won't perform without Bony anyway!

Angrily, SAM turns and yanks the door inwards to leave, and ALICE-MIRANDA tumbles into the barn.

TOM and SAM stare down at her. As ALICE-MIRANDA staggers up, TOM kicks the barn door shut and looms over her.

TOM
Well, well, it's you. Get into that stall, you nosy little girl!

ALICE-MIRANDA looks left and right. SAM stands with folded arms, blocking the exit. No escape.

BONAPARTE
(whinnying)

ALICE-MIRANDA backs into the stall and TOM <CLICKS> it shut.

In despair, ALICE-MIRANDA looks up at the tall wooden gate. There are no gaps, it's too high to climb and there's no room underneath.

TOM
That'll keep you out of the way!

However, he's forgotten BONAPARTE'S loyalty to ALICE-MIRANDA. BONAPARTE <SNORTS> angrily and rears up on his hind legs.

TOM (CONT'D)
Whoa!

BONAPARTE
(furious whinny)
Not on my watch, Mister!

BONAPARTE knocks TOM down with a <THUD>.

TOM
(yelping)

BONAPARTE rears up wildly at SAM, who flings the barn door open and bolts off into the woods. TOM staggers up and stumbles out the door after her.

ALICE-MIRANDA
Bony!

BONAPARTE
I'll save you, Alice-Miranda!

BONAPARTE kicks in the stall. The door swings open and ALICE-MIRANDA rushes out and wraps her arms around BONAPARTE'S neck.

ALICE-MIRANDA
Oh, Bony, are you okay?

BONAPARTE <WHINNIES> affectionately.

ALICE-MIRANDA glances out the door into the dark woods. TOM and SAM are out of sight.

ALICE-MIRANDA (CONT'D)
I'd love to catch those thieves, but
we have to get you back to Popstar.
We can't have anyone sabotaging
the Queen's Grand Prix.

ALICE-MIRANDA mounts BONAPARTE and canters out of the stables.

SCENE 62: EXT. WINCHESTERFIELD EQUESTRIAN FIELD – MEANWHILE

The Queen's Grand Prix dressage event is underway. POPSTAR is bucking in the waiting area, clearly upset.

Then ALICE-MIRANDA arrives on BONAPARTE, who stops with a <SNORT> at the fence by the waiting area.

BONAPARTE
Popstar!

POPSTAR spots him and quietens, suddenly docile as a lamb.

POPSTAR

Thank goodness!

Her rider arrives, face covered by a dressage hat and veil. We can't make out who it is. The rider mounts and enters the equestrian field.

BONAPARTE

(calling)

Remember, if you're nervous
just . . . well you know what to do.

POPSTAR

(whinnying giggles)

POPSTAR performs her dressage perfectly with her mystery rider. The performance is sensational!

MISS HIGGINS ON P.A. SYSTEM

And the gold medal goes to . . .
Popstar!

CROWD

(cheering loudly)

MISS HIGGINS ON P.A. SYSTEM

Ridden perfectly by . . .

The mystery rider unveils herself.

CROWD

(gasping)

Everyone's shocked to see AUNTY GEE.

MISS HIGGINS ON P.A. SYSTEM (O.S.)

Queen Georgiana herself!

CROWD

(even louder cheers)

ALICE-MIRANDA and MILLIE are on the sidelines. They squeal with delight.

MARJORIE

Bother.

MARJORIE pushes past them, speaking into her watch, after AUNTY GEE and POPSTAR. AUNTY GEE winks at ALICE-MIRANDA as she passes, and ALICE-MIRANDA waves back.

AUNTY GEE
Thank you Alice-Miranda. I feel
like my old self again!

MILLIE eyes her friend suspiciously.

MILLIE
Alice-Miranda, you organised this?

ALICE-MIRANDA
I made some small suggestions.

ALICE-MIRANDA shrugs, a small smile playing on her lips.

ALICE-MIRANDA (CONT'D)
I'm just glad Aunty Gee got to ride
Popstar in her own event.

We PULL OUT to a wide shot of the fair, with the sky above it colouring with streaks of pink.

ACT
3

SCENE 63: EXT. GRANNY VALENTINA'S COTTAGE – DAY

WIDE on GRANNY VALENTINA'S cottage.

Laughter intermingles with <CHRISTMAS MUSIC>. The sun beats down – it's summer. Birds sing in the trees and butterflies flitter amongst the flowers.

MILLIE/JACINTA (O.S.)
(laughing)

SCENE 64: EXT. GRANNY VALENTINA'S COTTAGE – GARDEN – DAY

ALICE-MIRANDA, MILLIE and JACINTA are having a picnic under a tree with AUNTY GEE and GRANNY VALENTINA in the beautiful garden.

There's an open picnic basket and a picnic lunch spread out.

ALICE-MIRANDA, MILLIE and JACINTA are lying on the grass idly weaving friendship bracelets from daisies.

JACINTA

It's so strange that the police never caught the horse thieves. Or the jewel thief.

MILLIE

It's like they did some weird vanishing trick. Poof!

MILLIE does a flourish like a magician – to indicate disappearing.

ALICE-MIRANDA

(reflective nod)

Right. It's curious that we suddenly have two unsolved thefts. Jewel theft and horse theft. I wonder if they could be connected . . .

She twirls a strand of hair thoughtfully.

JACINTA

I don't see how.

ALICE-MIRANDA

At least Bony and Popstar are safe.

(quietly)

They're hidden at Fayle School – together, of course. Just in case the thieves come back.

AUNTY GEE and GRANNY VALENTINA are sitting on a picnic rug.

GRANNY VALENTINA

Just like Gee is hiding here. Shame, but there's been even more of those nasty emails.

AUNTY GEE

The police have been completely unable to trace any of them. Mysterious indeed.

AUNTY GEE looks worried for a moment but puts on a brave face.

AUNTY GEE (CONT'D)
On a happier note, have you girls been naughty or nice?

The girls think . . .

GRANNY VALENTINA
Christmas is coming!

GIRLS
Christmas!/Ooh!/Of course!

Just then, MARJORIE and LLOYD hurry into the garden. MARJORIE holds an iPad.

MARJORIE
I'm afraid there's been some unpleasant news headlines from home this morning.

Everyone looks up, worried.

MARJORIE (CONT'D)
(reading)
'Queen Georgiana and crown jewels missing. Monarchy crumbling. Unconfirmed sightings on cruise liner and at country fair.'

LLOYD
(over her shoulder)
Don't forget this one: 'Why does Queen Gee neglect her people?' Shameful!

AUNTY GEE is shaken and GRANNY VALENTINA is too.

GRANNY VALENTINA
How do the newspapers know about the crown jewels? We kept their theft top secret. Strictly Code Black.

MARJORIE
Anybody could have spotted Her Majesty at the fair, however.

AUNTY GEE shakes her head and sighs deeply.

AUNTY GEE
I can't win. If I hide away I'm
neglecting my duties, but if I go
out in public I'm a target for
thieves, villains and bad press.

GRANNY VALENTINA puts a comforting hand on her arm.

GRANNY VALENTINA
Try not to let them upset you,
Gee.

AUNTY GEE
Oh, Val, I don't know what to do
and a monarch isn't a monarch
without her judgement.

She stands and brushes the grass from her dress. She looks weary and surprisingly old.

AUNTY GEE (CONT'D)
Maybe . . . maybe it's time for me
to step aside. Leave it all to Freddy.

The girls share a horrified glance.

ALICE-MIRANDA/MILLIE/JACINTA

(gasping)

ALICE-MIRANDA

But, Aunty Gee, everybody loves you.

AUNTY GEE shrugs.

AUNTY GEE

No Queen can rule forever.

MARJORIE steps forward.

MARJORIE

(clearing throat)

Your Majesty, your Silver Jubilee celebrations are on the calendar for December.

AUNTY GEE

Yes?

MARJORIE

With all this drama I suggest we cancel the Royal Silver Jubilee Ball.

This is not a popular suggestion with AUNTY GEE, GRANNY VALENTINA or the girls.

MILLIE

No way! Never! Wait, what's a Silver Jubilee?

ALICE-MIRANDA

It means Aunty Gee's been Queen for twenty-five years.

MARJORIE

Nobody knows who might be in the crowd.

LLOYD stands sombrely, beside his fiancé. But GRANNY VALENTINA reacts.

GRANNY VALENTINA

Phooey to that!

ALICE-MIRANDA springs up.

ALICE-MIRANDA

Yes, phooey to that! Why not hold the ball at our school? It's hidden away from everything. You can be the special guest.

JACINTA springs up to join ALICE-MIRANDA.

JACINTA

It'll be a Silver Jubilee Christmas Ball. With a royal guest!

MILLIE leaps up, too, exuberant, flinging daisies into the air like confetti.

MILLIE

Have you ever heard of anything so wonderful?!

MILLIE and JACINTA both dance with delight. MARJORIE winces.

MARJORIE

Your Majesty, I'm afraid it's too dangerous.

As AUNTY GEE considers, ALICE-MIRANDA drops to her knees at AUNTY GEE'S feet.

ALICE-MIRANDA

Please, Aunty Gee, please! We have a state-of-the-art security system at school. Miss Grimm made sure of that! And the students can organise everything.

AUNTY GEE looks at everyone, then down at ALICE-MIRANDA. She shrugs and smiles.

AUNTY GEE

How can I say no to you, Alice-Miranda?

ALICE-MIRANDA leaps up, overjoyed.

ALICE-MIRANDA

Yes!

MILLIE/JACINTA
(cheering)

MARJORIE flinches. She doesn't want this stress.

LLOYD
Never mind, darling. I can take care of security.

ALICE-MIRANDA
We'll start tomorrow!

CUT TO:

SCENE 65: INT. WINCHESTERFIELD-DOWNSFORDVALE CLASSROOM – THE NEXT DAY

CLOSE ON ALICE-MIRANDA reading from a list.

ALICE-MIRANDA
Lights, music, catering, decorations and a special throne for Her Majesty. There's a job for everyone.

PULL OUT TO REVEAL students gathered around her, listening, including MILLIE, IVORY, JACINTA, LUCAS and some Fayle boys, ALETHEA and ASHIMA and CAPRICE.

ALICE-MIRANDA (CONT'D)
Alethea and Ashima will be coordinating it all.

ALICE-MIRANDA passes the list to ASHIMA, but ALETHEA snatches the list first.

ALETHEA stands up and tosses her hair about, extravagantly.

ALETHEA
To be precise, I'll be coordinating it with my assistant.

ASHIMA smiles and shrugs. She doesn't care.

ALETHEA (CONT'D)
So, any volunteers for the catering?

CAPRICE and JACINTA both put up their hands.

When they notice each other, they quickly put down their hands and look away, frowning.

ALICE-MIRANDA notices, tilts her head.

ALICE-MIRANDA
We're going to need both of your amazing baking skills.

JACINTA and CAPRICE share a quick look, feeling proud. Do we have an alliance?

ALETHEA
Next item: music.

TRANSITION TO:

SCENE 66: INT. WINCHESTERFIELD-DOWNSFORDVALE SCHOOL HALL – NIGHT

MONTAGE:
– <CHRISTMAS MUSIC> plays. All students are wearing Santa hats and having fun.
– Boys and girls are decorating a large Christmas tree with baubles and tinsel.

– IVORY hangs baubles from her ears as earrings; the others laugh.
– MILLIE and SUSANNAH are wrapping a long string of tinsel around and around the big tree.

ALETHEA wanders past, distracted.

ALETHEA
Tree, lights, music . . .

ASHIMA hurries behind her with her clipboard.

ASHIMA
Look out, Alethea!

ALETHEA'S so preoccupied she gets entwined in the tinsel that MILLIE and SUSANNAH are wrapping round the tree. It tightens around her ankles and she falls, rattling the tree, and with baubles raining down on her.

ALETHEA
Argh! I think I broke a nail.

ASHIMA helps her untangle herself. She has some pine needles in her hair.

– Boys and girls use hammers and nails to put together a wooden throne. ALETHEA stops one of them.

ALETHEA (CONT'D)

Who doesn't know how to use a hammer? Watch and learn.

She bangs her finger with the hammer.

ALETHEA (CONT'D)

(furiously)

Ouch!

– Students carry piles of boxes through the hall.

ALETHEA (CONT'D)

Be careful!

She steps backwards and trips on a bauble. At that moment CAPRICE and JACINTA enter with a sample trays of food – individual croquembouches dressed as little snowmen.

JACINTA

Do you like my . . .

JACINTA looks at CAPRICE.

CAPRICE

You mean our Christmas croquembouches?

ALETHEA collides with the tray and they go tumbling all over her, covering her with sticky icing and decorations.

CAPRICE (CONT'D)

Sorry, Alethea.

ALETHEA spins around.

ALETHEA

Now you've ruined my hair!

She then steps backwards and again stumbles into the Christmas tree. The students rush to steady it. Disaster averted! Then the star falls SLOW MOTION in a trajectory towards ALETHEA'S head. At the last moment, ASHIMA catches it, saving ALETHEA from danger.

ASHIMA

Ugh!

ASHIMA leads ALETHEA away, arm around ALETHEA'S shoulder.

ASHIMA (CONT'D)

How about taking a break, Alethea?

– The Christmas lights are finally hung. ASHIMA switches them on. They flicker, then sparkle in Christmas colours.

STUDENTS

(gasping in delight)

– The tree's finally decorated. Calmly, ASHIMA hands SUSANNAH the star. SUSANNAH reaches high from a ladder to place it on top. The surrounding girls and boys <APPLAUD>.

ALETHEA is sitting down with her arm in a bandage, and a lump on her forehead, with snowman icing all over her. She is humbled.

ASHIMA
(to ALETHEA)
How are you feeling?

TRANSITION TO:

SCENE 67: INT. WINCHESTERFIELD-DOWNSFORDVALE LIBRARY – DAY

ALICE-MIRANDA is making a display of AUNTY GEE'S family tree, mounting pictures on a board.

At the top it has pictures of brothers KING HENRY and KING ARTHUR. Below HENRY is his son – LLOYD'S FATHER – then LLOYD. Below ARTHUR are AUNTY GEE, her son FREDDY and her grandchildren, the PRINCES.

ALICE-MIRANDA
Lots of students are interested in the monarchy. This family tree should make it clearer.

She attaches a photo of AUNTY GEE wearing the crown, holding the sceptre and orb.

MILLIE and JACINTA are watching her, curious. JACINTA traces a line from Georgiana to Freddy.

JACINTA
So . . . Aunty Gee's son Freddy is next in line for the throne. He's the twins' dad.

ALICE-MIRANDA
Yes. And after him, the twins. Prince Edgar is the oldest.

MILLIE/JACINTA
(laughing)

MILLIE points to the photo of the PRINCES. They are young and wearing fake moustaches.

MILLIE
Look at them. Pranking already!

On another branch of the 'tree' is a photo of LLOYD. He's in a silly hat.

JACINTA
That's a funny one of Lord Lloyd. Where did you find these pictures?

ALICE-MIRANDA

In the library. Aunty Gee went to school here, remember. That's when she met Granny.

MILLIE

Yeah. Like eons ago.

CLOSE ON a fun old photo: AUNTY GEE and GRANNY VALENTINA as ten-year-olds at the Winchesterfield Fair, eating fairy floss.

ALICE-MIRANDA/MILLIE/JACINTA

(laughing)

MILLIE

And Lloyd went to Fayle for a term, like the princes are.

The photos have the royal crest embossed on them. JACINTA runs her finger across one.

JACINTA

The royal crest.

ALICE-MIRANDA

It means the photos are genuine.

MILLIE scrunches up her nose, confused, studying the display.

MILLIE

Wait. If the monarchy passes from parent to child, why didn't King Henry's oldest son become King? Then Lloyd?

She traces the line from KING HENRY down to LLOYD via his father.

ALICE-MIRANDA

That was big news, Millie!

ANGLE ON the photos of brothers HENRY and ARTHUR. ALICE-MIRANDA points.

ALICE-MIRANDA (O.S.) (CONT'D)

King Henry was in love with a woman called Evelyn and he wanted to marry her. But she was divorced so he had to abdicate.

JACINTA

What does that mean?!

ALICE-MIRANDA

That means he gave up the throne
to his younger brother, Arthur.
Arthur was Aunty Gee's dad. And
Henry wasn't King any more.

JACINTA'S miffed.

JACINTA

Why? Divorce isn't a crime. It's
actually quite common.

ALICE-MIRANDA

All this was years ago when the
church and the monarchy didn't
approve of divorce. Times change.

JACINTA'S face falls, thinking of her parents.

JACINTA

(sighing)

ALICE-MIRANDA

I've been looking for the
abdication document to help

everyone understand, but it's been missing for years.

She frowns as she twirls her hair.

ALICE-MIRANDA (CONT'D)
Curious.

TRANSITION TO:

SCENE 68: EXT. WINCHESTERFIELD-DOWNSFORDVALE SCHOOL – DAY

It's the day of the Royal Christmas Ball. We PAN across the school which is sparkling with decorations.

ALICE-MIRANDA (O.S.)
We're ready for the Royal Christmas Ball!

SCENE 69: INT./EXT. WINCHESTERFIELD HOUSE – AFTERNOON

VARIOUS DORMS: SUSANNAH and IVORY, in ball gowns, admire each other in a mirror. They speak at the same time, then laugh.

IVORY/SUSANNAH

Hey, we look awesome!

ALETHEA and ASHIMA, also in ball gowns, also look in the mirror.

ALETHEA

I'm ready to dance with a prince.

She flounces her hair. So does ASHIMA.

ASHIMA

Me too.

ALETHEA

Lucky there's two of them. But I've
got the older one, okay.

They share a smile. It seems the head prefect and vice prefect are finally friends.

ALETHEA/ASHIMA

(giggling)

OUTSIDE: The PRINCES and LLOYD trot up on decorated ponies.

From the PRINCES' POV we see the girls look out dorm windows and giggle.

PAN ACROSS the windows. Girls' voices waft around in the breeze.

STUDENTS

So handsome!/Which one is which?/Who cares?/I'll dance with either./I hope I can!

The PRINCES grin at the attention.

PRINCE LOUIS

(calling out)

We'll dance with all of you!

GIRLS

(squealing)

ALICE-MIRANDA'S DORM: ALICE-MIRANDA, MILLIE and JACINTA are dressed for the ball. They look stunning. ALICE-MIRANDA'S hair is in a bun.

ALICE-MIRANDA

That dress is perfect on you, Jacinta.

CAPRICE steps into the dorm wearing the same dress as JACINTA. Shock! They glare at each other, both upset.

JACINTA

One of us has to change!

CAPRICE steps back, remembering JACINTA'S rage at the fair. She looks uncertain.

CAPRICE

But I don't have another dress.

JACINTA

Me either. And my dad bought this dress for me.

Awkward! ALICE-MIRANDA steps between them, breaking the stalemate. She's thinking on her feet.

ALICE-MIRANDA

Caprice, I have a lovely silk sash in royal blue.

She rushes to get it from her wardrobe.

ALICE-MIRANDA (CONT'D)
It would suit you perfectly. And make your dress look different to Jacinta's.

More awkward silence. CAPRICE shrugs. ALICE-MIRANDA holds it up.

ALICE-MIRANDA (CONT'D)
See?

CAPRICE looks in the mirror.

CAPRICE
Well. I guess I could try it.

JACINTA melts.

JACINTA
Thanks, Caprice.
(on impulse)
Maybe . . . could we start from the beginning as if we'd only just met?

CAPRICE considers, then she sticks out her hand.

CAPRICE

I'm Caprice Radford, your new roommate.

JACINTA grins and shakes her hand.

JACINTA

Jacinta Headlington-Bear. I'm sure we'll get on famously.

CAPRICE

And FYI, my parents are divorced. So I know how it feels. I – I don't know why I was so mean to you. I think I was angry and it got out of hand.

CAPRICE and JACINTA share a tentative smile – this truce is new and fragile.

SCENE 70: INT. WINCHESTERFIELD-DOWNSFORVALE – MISS GRIMM'S SECURITY ROOM – MEANWHILE

LLOYD and MARJORIE step into the room. They ogle the video screens and audio equipment.

MARJORIE

The girl was right about the state-of-the-art security. There are cameras all over the school.

On the screens we see various shots of the school, the stables, the hallways, the dining hall, etc.

LLOYD

Excellent, leave me in charge, my sweet. I won't let you down.

MARJORIE looks uncertain, but is convinced by LLOYD'S words.

MARJORIE

I do need to stick close to Her Majesty.

She taps her watch.

MARJORIE (CONT'D)

Call me if you need anything.

She exits in haste as LLOYD peruses the screens.

SCENE 71: INT. FAYLE SCHOOL – MEANWHILE

In the corridor, MR LIPP frantically rounds up the boys into a line to board the bus to Winchesterfield-Downsfordvale.

MR LIPP (O.S.)

All boys to the bus! Hurry up now . . . Christmas Balls wait for no man. Or boy.

SCENE 72: INT. FAYLE SCHOOL HALL – MEANWHILE

Hustle and bustle inside the hall. Every boy has put effort into looking extra spick.

MR LIPP

(calling)

Form an orderly queue. No hijinks or goofing around please!

However, LUCAS isn't happy with his jacket, which he's outgrown – he shows MR LIPP his short sleeves.

LUCAS

Mr Lipp. My jacket's too small.

MR LIPP

Goodness, Lucas, talk about
leaving things to the last minute!
Get one from the costume room.

LUCAS

Thanks, Mr Lipp.

MR LIPP

But don't be tardy. The bus leaves
at five pm with you or without
you. Oh my!

SCENE 73: EXT. WINCHESTERFIELD COUNTRY LANES – MEANWHILE

AUNTY GEE and GRANNY VALENTINA race down the country lanes in an ordinary mini, which

AUNTY GEE is driving at top speed, in full evening dress that includes the ruby tiara that ALICE-MIRANDA saved on the cruise. Clearly the event has cheered AUNTY GEE up.

AUNTY GEE/GRANNY VALENTINA
Woo hoo!

The BODYGUARD is in the back seat turning white, hands gripping the seat.

BODYGUARD
Argh . . .

SCENE 74: INT. SCHOOL CORRIDORS/ DORM – SOON AFTER

When they arrive, AUNTY GEE and GRANNY VALENTINA hurry along the corridor to take a look at the dorm they once shared.

GRANNY VALENTINA
I remember these halls so well.

AUNTY GEE
Do you remember running

through them to get to bed before
lights out?

GRANNY VALENTINA
(a little embarrassed)
Oh, yes.

As they reach the dorms, IVORY, ASHIMA, ALETHEA and SUSANNAH poke their heads out of their dorms.

The girls squeal with delight to see AUNTY GEE in her royal outfit. AUNTY GEE twirls for them. Then they go into ALICE-MIRANDA'S dorm . . .

ALICE-MIRANDA
Aunty Gee. Granny! You both
look stunning.

She hugs them both. Just then, MILLIE comes racing in with her iPad. She reads out some headlines.

MILLIE
Aunty Gee, I'm sorry but these are
the latest news headlines.

(reading)
'Queen is not Queen. Unsigned document found. King Henry's abdication was not legal!'

AUNTY GEE is shocked. She sits heavily onto a bed. ALICE-MIRANDA sits beside her, along with GRANNY VALENTINA.

ALICE-MIRANDA
Oh, Aunty Gee! It can't be true.

AUNTY GEE touches her key necklace for comfort.

AUNTY GEE
It's not. Well, I don't think it is. Father always said there was a legal document, but he hid it away for safe-keeping.

ALICE-MIRANDA
Can you think where it might be?

AUNTY GEE shakes her head sadly.

AUNTY GEE
He hid it too well.

SCENE 75: INT. COSTUME ROOM FAYLE COSTUME ROOM – MEANWHILE

LUCAS has found a great jacket. He puts it on and checks himself in the mirror. Nice! Then he spots something twinkling green under the lights. It's hidden amongst the costume jewellery used for theatrical productions.

He rakes through the jewellery, and pulls out something.

CLOSE ON one of AUNT CHARLOTTE'S emerald earrings. LUCAS studies it.

LUCAS

This looks just like Charlotte's
earring from the ship.

He searches further and gasps at what he sees . . .

SCENE 76: INT. WINCHESTERFIELD-DOWNSFORDVALE CORRIDOR/FAYLE COSTUME ROOM/MISS GRIMM'S SECURITY ROOM

INTERCUT:

CORRIDOR: Girls are thronging through corridors in their gowns, waiting for the ball to start.

GIRLS
(excited hubbub)

The phone in the corridor <RINGS>. JACINTA picks it up.

JACINTA
Grimthorpe House, Jacinta speaking.

SPLIT SCREEN:

WINCHESTERFIELD-DOWNSFORDVALE and FAYLE:

LUCAS
Jacinta . . .?

JACINTA
Hi, Lucas.
(coy)
Are you coming over?

LUCAS

Soon. I can't wait to see you, but right now could you find Alice-Miranda? It's urgent.

JACINTA

Sure.

She moves the phone away from her mouth.

JACINTA (CONT'D)

(bellowing)

Alice-Miranda! Phone!

ALICE-MIRANDA hurries over and takes the phone.

LUCAS

Alice-Miranda, I need you to come to Fayle ASAP.

REVEAL: LUCAS holds the glinting royal orb in his hand.

SCENE 77: INT. MISS GRIMM'S OFFICE/ SECURITY ROOM BEHIND OFFICE

MISS GRIMM'S SECURITY ROOM: LLOYD is distracted by one of the many screens – ALICE-MIRANDA'S whispering to MILLIE.

He frowns and flicks an audio switch.

ALICE-MIRANDA
(whispering)
. . . missing jewels . . .

LLOYD looks puzzled.

LLOYD
Missing jewels?!

ALICE-MIRANDA
(whispering)
. . . secret tunnel . . .

LLOYD
Secret tunnel? What shenanigans are they up to now?

OFFICE: ALICE-MIRANDA and MILLIE enter MISS GRIMM'S office, heading for the secret tunnel to Fayle.

MILLIE
Lucky we know the fast way to Fayle.

SECURITY ROOM: The girls come bowling into the security room where LLOYD is, then see him and stop dead. LLOYD is charming and breezy.

LLOYD
Hi, girls, I'm managing the security room for Marjorie.

ALICE-MIRANDA
Oh, I see.

She shares a despairing look with MILLIE. They don't want to enter the secret tunnel with LLOYD present, revealing it.

ALICE-MIRANDA (CONT'D)
Okay then we'll just . . .

ALICE-MIRANDA backs away towards the door, but trips over an open backpack, knocking it over.

ALICE-MIRANDA (CONT'D)
Oops!

The contents spill out onto the floor for them all to see. Tubes of make-up, brushes and two latex masks!

CLOSE ON the two masks. One looks like PETER, the porter, one like TOM, the horse trainer.

LLOYD hurries over and starts shoving things back into the bag. ALICE-MIRANDA turns to LLOYD in horror.

ALICE-MIRANDA (CONT'D)
Wait, this mask looks like the jewel thief!

MILLIE
And this one's the horse thief!

LLOYD jumps into action, looming over the girls.

CLOSE ON ALICE-MIRANDA as she closes her eyes briefly.

FLASHBACK to PETER looming over her in the same position as LLOYD, when she was in the laundry trolley.

FLASHBACK to TOM looming over her in the stable.

ALICE-MIRANDA opens her eyes.

LLOYD

I have no idea what you're talking about. What are you doing in here anyway?

ALICE-MIRANDA'S eyes glance towards the door to the secret tunnel. MILLIE clocks what ALICE-MIRANDA'S thinking.

LLOYD (CONT'D)

You've breached security!

The girls scoot towards the door to the secret tunnel. They share a look.

ALICE-MIRANDA

Oh no. Don't lock us in that . . . cupboard!

They step backwards towards the door. Thinking it's

truly a cupboard, LLOYD grabs the door handle and yanks it open. Only darkness inside.

LLOYD

Perfect.

The girls back into the secret tunnel. LLOYD slams the door on them and turns the key, locking it.

LLOYD (CONT'D)

Stupid brats.

SCENE 78: INT. SECRET TUNNEL TO FAYLE SCHOOL – CONTINUOUS

It's no cupboard. In the dim light that leads to the tunnel, the girls laugh silently.

MILLIE

(whispering)

He's the stupid one. He thinks we're locked in a cupboard.

The girls lift their ball gowns, kick off their ballet flats and hold onto them as they race down the tunnel.

MILLIE (CONT'D)

Was Lloyd behind everything that's upset Aunty Gee? The thefts, the threats, the headlines?

ALICE-MIRANDA nods.

ALICE-MIRANDA

Yes, but what's his motive? There's a lot we still need to figure out, but I'm sure the jewels will help!

They arrive at the few stairs to the costume room and meet LUCAS with the royal orb. They're puffing with exhaustion.

ALICE-MIRANDA (CONT'D)

(puffing)

The royal orb! Where did you find it?

SCENE 79: INT. COSTUME ROOM FAYLE – MOMENTS AFTER

LUCAS has laid out the rest of the jewels, including assorted earrings, bracelets and watches.

ALICE-MIRANDA picks up the sceptre.

LUCAS

I don't know what they're doing here.

CLOSE ON ALICE-MIRANDA as she closes her eyes briefly. FLASHBACK to AUNTY GEE on the cruise deck.

AUNTY GEE

He was the head of the drama club in his day.

ALICE-MIRANDA opens her eyes.

ALICE-MIRANDA

Lloyd went to Fayle. Maybe he thought hiding the jewels among costume jewels was clever.

LUCAS

Lloyd?!

ALICE-MIRANDA and MILLIE nod.

LUCAS (CONT'D)

Well . . .

(smiling)

He didn't count on my jacket being too small.

ALICE-MIRANDA takes the royal orb from LUCAS and turns it in her hand. CLOSE ON her finger running over a small keyhole.

ALICE-MIRANDA

He's planning something big, and what better time to strike than at the ball tonight?

She passes the orb back to LUCAS.

ALICE-MIRANDA (CONT'D)

We have to warn Aunty Gee! We should bring the jewels as proof. But the ball starts at six . . .

They look at the clock on the wall showing 5:58.

ALICE-MIRANDA (CONT'D)

Here's the plan . . .

SCENE 80: INT. WINCHESTERFIELD-DOWNSFORDVALE SCHOOL – MAIN HALL – TWO MINUTES LATER

A similar clock on the wall ticks over to six pm.

Music plays, heralding the start of the ball. The Christmas lights twinkle. There are small tables dotted about with bunches of Christmas bush on them. Red candles are also placed around.

Beautifully dressed girls and boys enter the hall.

STUDENTS
(laughing and chatting)

Various adults join the students: CECELIA and HUGH, LAWRENCE and CHARLOTTE, MISS GRIMM and ALDOUS GRUMP, AMBROSIA (on her phone), GRANNY VALENTINA, MR LIPP, MISS HIGGINS and CONSTABLE DERBY.

ADULTS
(quiet hubbub)

MISS HIGGINS

When do you think the Queen will arrive?

MR LIPP nervously adjusts his collar and tie.

MR LIPP

She should be here any minute, unless something's gone wrong! Do you think something's gone wrong?

SCENE 81: INT. WINCHESTERFIELD-DOWNSFORDVALE SCHOOL – CORRIDOR/FAYLE SCHOOL CORRIDOR

WINCHESTERFIELD: The phone in the corridor <RINGS>. ALETHEA answers it.

ALETHEA

Alice-Miranda? Sure.

She throws down the phone and runs off.

ALETHEA (CONT'D)

(OTT flirty)

Prince Edgar! Prince Louis! You're wanted.

PRINCE EDGAR takes the phone and the boys listen together.

SPLIT SCREEN: FAYLE and WINCHESTERFIELD-DOWNSFORDVALE

ALICE-MIRANDA

I need you to delay the start of the ball. How many pranks have you got?

PRINCE EDGAR

Heaps. But everyone's already here.

PRINCE LOUIS

Except Granny.

ALICE-MIRANDA

Use every prank – so long as you

don't hurt anyone. I'll be as quick as I can.

The PRINCES smile wickedly.

PRINCE EDGAR

You asked for it.

ALICE-MIRANDA

One other thing . . .

The PRINCES smile.

SCENE 82: EXT. THE FIELDS BETWEEN THE SCHOOLS/WINCHESTERFIELD-DOWNSFORDVALE SCHOOL HALL

INTERCUT:

FAYLE PADDOCK: ALICE-MIRANDA arrives and quickly fastens a saddle onto BONAPARTE.

ALICE-MIRANDA

Bony, we have a royal mission!

She quickly mounts. POPSTAR <WHINNYS> a protest.

ALICE-MIRANDA (CONT'D)
Don't worry, Popstar, you have a part in this mission too.

She quickly steers BONAPARTE out the paddock gate and closes it and it <CLICKS> closed behind her.

BONAPARTE
It's alright, Popstar. Do what they say!

FIELDS: ALICE-MIRANDA gallops to Winchesterfield-Downsfordvale in evening gown and riding hat on BONAPARTE, who jumps a fence.

BONAPARTE (CONT'D)
What's the rush?

THE HALL: As the people mingle, the PRINCES roll out their first prank.

The music changes from <CHRISTMAS CAROLS> to <HARD ROCK>.

Onstage, at the school podium microphone, MISS GRIMM reacts in surprise.

MISS GRIMM
Oh. Must be a technical error.

Everyone covers their ears.

CROWD
(shocked hubbub)

MR LIPP
(shouts)
Boys, I said background music! Background! This isn't a teen disco.

The PRINCES – hidden under the audio table – high-five.

PRINCE LOUIS
It is now.

FIELDS: ALICE-MIRANDA holds on tight as BONAPARTE rides through. Sheep scatter. <BAA>.

ALICE-MIRANDA
Good boy, Bony!

THE HALL: The music has died down. MISS GRIMM takes the microphone to welcome the guests. She starts to speak, and her voice comes through the P.A. SYSTEM at a helium pitch.

MISS GRIMM

(high-pitched)

Good evening everyone,
I apologise for the –

CROWD

(laughing)

MISS GRIMM

(high-pitched)

Oh dear, another technical hitch.

MR LIPP'S hand goes to his head.

MR LIPP

Hitch? It's a disaster!

MISS GRIMM steps back. Still under the audio desk, the PRINCES high-five again.

PRINCE EDGAR

You ain't seen nothing yet.

FIELDS: MILLIE and LUCAS ride through the fields on POPSTAR; MILLIE clutching the laundry bag of jewellery.

LUCAS

Good girl, Popstar, just follow
your nose. We're going to meet
your best friend Bony . . .

FIELDS: ALICE-MIRANDA gallops on BONAPARTE towards her school.

THE HALL: The lights go out. Only candles flicker. Everyone gasps. The PRINCES, in bedsheets, rush through the hall.

PRINCE EDGAR/PRINCE LOUIS

We are the ghosts of Christmas
past.

CROWD

(screaming)

MISS GRIMM becomes more flustered.

MISS GRIMM

Attention, everyone! Whoever is behind these pranks will be seeing me in my office.

MR LIPP is having a comic meltdown.

MR LIPP

A complete, full-scale disaster!

He faints, only to be caught by LAWRENCE RIDLEY. He opens his eyes. At the sight of the movie star . . .

MR LIPP (CONT'D)

Oh my! You're that famous actor! Lawrence Ridley. And me . . . I'm not even wearing my best tie!

He faints again.

FIELDS: BONAPARTE leaps over a creek at speed.

Strands of ALICE-MIRANDA'S neatly-tied bun are flying loose.

ALICE-MIRANDA
(calling)
Faster, Bony, faster!

SCENE 83: INT. WINCHESTERFIELD-DOWNSFORDVALE SCHOOL HALL – SOON AFTER

All is finally calm and under control. The lights are on, Christmas music is playing. Guests gather around small tables that have glasses of soft drink on them.

CAPRICE and JACINTA sweep through the hall carrying extravagant trays of food.

From the stage, MISS GRIMM welcomes everyone again.

MISS GRIMM
After a bumpy start, I'd like to
finally welcome everyone to the
Royal Christmas Ball.

We'll begin with a speech from
an ex-student of Winchesterfield-
Downsfordvale . . .

CROWD
(excited murmurs)

MISS GRIMM
None other than our Silver Jubilee
Queen, Her Majesty, Georgiana
the First!

CROWD
(cheering)

Everyone raises their phones/cameras.

MISS GRIMM
Please, no photos, no social media.
The Queen is under tight security.

AUNTY GEE is ushered in by her BODYGUARD and sits on the special throne. GRANNY VALENTINA is close. Everyone <APPLAUDS>.

AUNTY GEE

Distinguished guests –

Suddenly, the music stops and the lights dim. Another prank?!

CROWD

(gasping)

In the audience, the PRINCES look at each other in surprise. It's not them. Then LLOYD'S voice is heard over the speakers.

LLOYD ON P.A. SYSTEM (O.S.)

Before you do, Aunt Georgiana . . .

Everyone looks around for the source of the voice. LLOYD appears suddenly and dramatically in a spotlight beside the throne.

LLOYD

You've all heard the news about
the abdication of King Henry
being illegal. I have here the very
document that proves it.

He waves his document.

LLOYD (CONT'D)

This is my father's abdication document. Unsigned! He never officially gave up the throne. This brings about the end of your reign, Aunty, and the beginning of mine.

There's stunned silence. The lights flicker back on.

AUNTY GEE is pale and looks small in her throne. She takes the document from LLOYD and scans it.

LLOYD (CONT'D)

As the oldest living descendant of King Henry, I am the rightful King.

GRANNY VALENTINA

This can't be true.

AUNTY GEE waves the document at GRANNY VALENTINA, who comes forwards to take it. AUNTY GEE is very distressed.

AUNTY GEE

I think it might be, Val. He's right, there's no signature.

GRANNY VALENTINA examines the document.

CLOSE ON the formal-looking document. The signature is missing. AUNTY GEE touches the key at her neck.

AUNTY GEE (CONT'D)

It means my whole life has been a lie.

Slowly, AUNTY GEE takes off her tiara. She stands, and hands it to LLOYD . . .

. . . when ALICE-MIRANDA, on BONAPARTE, bursts into the hall.

ALICE-MIRANDA

(hollering)

Stop! It's not true, Aunty Gee!

BONAPARTE skids to a stop. ALICE-MIRANDA leaps off and runs to the stage.

She's lost a shoe and her hair is dishevelled, but she doesn't notice as she steps onstage.

BONAPARTE turns and wanders outside, though not before swiping a piece of carrot from a canapé tray sitting on a table.

ALICE-MIRANDA (CONT'D)
Lloyd's the jewel thief and the horse thief! And a very bad person, it seems.

LLOYD, who holds the tiara, looks hurt.

LLOYD
Why would you say something so terrible?

GRANNY VALENTINA
Let Alice-Miranda speak!

ALICE-MIRANDA
May I see that document, Granny?

GRANNY VALENTINA hands her LLOYD'S document. ALICE-MIRANDA scans the document.

Everyone's waiting with bated breath.

ALICE-MIRANDA (CONT'D)
Aha . . .

CLOSE ON the document. Then on ALICE-MIRANDA'S face as she briefly closes her eyes. Remembering . . .

FLASHBACK to JACINTA running her finger across the royal crest on a photo.

ALICE-MIRANDA'S eyes spring open.

ALICE-MIRANDA (CONT'D)
You should pay attention to details, Lloyd. There's no royal crest. Every real royal document has one. This must be a fake.

LLOYD snatches the document from ALICE-MIRANDA.

LLOYD
Oh puh-lease, she's only a child. What would she know?

MILLIE and LUCAS arrive on POPSTAR with the jewels. They drop the laundry bag with a <CLANK> at ALICE-MIRANDA'S feet.

POPSTAR exits.

ALICE-MIRANDA
(whispering to MILLIE and LUCAS)
Nice timing.
(loudly to everyone)
If anyone needs further proof, we
found the jewellery Lloyd stole!

MILLIE and LUCAS empty out the jewels onto the stage. A cascade of colour sparkles in front of AUNTY GEE'S throne. Everyone stares in amazement.

The royal orb rolls to LUCAS'S feet. He picks it up.

CROWD
(gasping)

HUGH
(from audience)
My watch!

AUNT CHARLOTTE
(from audience)
My earrings!

AUNTY GEE touches the key necklace around her neck in surprise.

AUNTY GEE
My goodness!

CLOSE ON AUNTY GEE'S little key.

CLOSE ON ALICE-MIRANDA staring at it. Then her eyes close briefly.

FLASHBACK to AUNTY GEE reciting the rhyme about the mysterious key necklace to ALICE-MIRANDA.

AUNTY GEE (CONT'D)
'If royal trouble comes to be, the
proof is under lock and key.'

ALICE-MIRANDA'S eyes spring open again.

LOSE ON the orb, which LUCAS is clutching. ALICE-MIRANDA'S eyes widen.

ALICE-MIRANDA

(quietly)

Aunty Gee, I think I know where your father hid the real document. May I borrow the key he gave you?

AUNTY GEE looks at ALICE-MIRANDA shrewdly, realising she's up to something.

AUNTY GEE

Of course, dear.

She hands over the key on its chain.

ALICE-MIRANDA

Lucas, can you pass me the royal orb?

ANGLE ON the royal orb that LUCAS clasps. He hands it to her. ALICE-MIRANDA fits the key into the orb's keyhole and . . .

<CLICK!> The orb opens to reveal an old piece of

paper, rolled and tied. GRANNY VALENTINA'S jaw drops open.

GRANNY VALENTINA

Alice-Miranda!

ALICE-MIRANDA delicately unrolls it, showing the document to everyone. CLOSE ON the royal crest.

ALICE-MIRANDA

This is the original abdication
document, signed and complete
with royal crest.

LLOYD

(agitated)

That's no proof of anything!

AUNTY GEE stands up and takes the tiara from LLOYD'S hand. She seems taller and more confident.

AUNTY GEE

I don't care if you're my nephew –
threatening my reign is treason!

ALICE-MIRANDA speaks to the audience.

ALICE-MIRANDA

Who would you rather believe:
Queen Georgiana or a thief?

LLOYD

I'm not a thief!

The lights go out again. A spotlight in the audience illuminates the PRINCES each wearing a latex mask. One is PETER and one is TOM.

EVERYONE

(gasping)

The PRINCES peel off the masks.

ALICE-MIRANDA

Lloyd had these masks in his bag.

The lights come on again. The Guard steps up to LLOYD.

ALICE-MIRANDA (CONT'D)

You stole the crown jewels and

sabotaged the Queen's Grand Prix. And you sent her threatening emails and fed false stories to the media. You made the Queen doubt herself. All so you could steal her throne and become King yourself!

AUNTY GEE

(calling)

Arrest him!

MARJORIE hurries onstage. She looks grim.

MARJORIE

(nodding)

Of course, Your Majesty.

An upset MARJORIE handcuffs her own fiancé.

MARJORIE (CONT'D)

How could you, Lloyd?! Forgery. Theft. And treason! Who are you?

She hustles LLOYD offstage.

MR LIPP reprises his role from the Fayle drama club.

MR LIPP

And now, the show must go on!

Dance music and the light show start. A few couples start to dance, including LAWRENCE and AUNT CHARLOTTE who have eyes for nobody else.

AUNTY GEE, though shaken, sits back on the throne. ALICE-MIRANDA hugs her and gives her the sceptre.

ALICE-MIRANDA

It's all over, Aunty Gee. You don't need to be afraid anymore – you're the rightful Queen.

AUNTY GEE clutches her ruby tiara. She places it on ALICE-MIRANDA'S head, and tucks her few untidy curls under it.

AUNTY GEE

I'd like you to wear this tonight. It should be worn by a brave and

noble person and you, my sweet
child, are both.

(calling)

Now, pump up the music!

The music rises. disco lights dance about. The Christmas decorations sparkle. Everyone rushes onto the dance floor.

ALICE-MIRANDA

Shall we dance?

She kicks off her one shoe and leads AUNTY GEE onto the dance floor.

ALETHEA approaches PRINCE EDGAR and offers her hand.

ALETHEA

Would you do me the pleasure?

Edgar smiles, slightly charmed.

PRINCE EDGAR

Sure.

ALETHEA

You'd better not step on my toes.

PRINCE LOUIS approaches ASHIMA.

PRINCE LOUIS

Dance?

ASHIMA FLUSHES.

ASHIMA

I–I'd love to.

IVORY, SUSANNAH and CAPRICE dance, with IVORY doing some cool moves in her wheelchair. MISS GRIMM and MR LIPP dance with the students. AUNTY GEE dances with GRANNY VALENTINA.

AMBROSIA notices her daughter standing alone and approaches.

AMBROSIA

(emotional)

Honey, I'm so sorry about

everything. I'm not a perfect
mother . . .

JACINTA

Yeah . . . no.

AMBROSIA

. . . but I want you to know
I always love you even when I mess
up.

She wipes away a tear. JACINTA smiles.

JACINTA

I love you, too, Mum.

Then AMBROSIA'S phone rings with the now familiar <RINGTONE>. She glances at the screen.

AMBROSIA

Sorry, honey, I have to –

As JACINTA glares at her, AMBROSIA hesitates. Then she hits a button and puts her phone away.

AMBROSIA (CONT'D)

Shall we dance?

JACINTA is overjoyed, but tries to act cool.

JACINTA

Okay.

They dance together a little awkwardly. Then LUCAS arrives.

LUCAS

May I cut in?

JACINTA grins and her mother smiles. JACINTA and LUCAS dance with looks reminiscent of AUNT CHARLOTTE and LAWRENCE.

BONAPARTE sticks his head through a window, wearing reindeer antlers, and eats another carrot stick from a canapé tray. POPSTAR also sticks her head in and licks up some red cabbage. <MUNCH!>.

POPSTAR

Not loving the music.

BONAPARTE

At least the food's good.

In the centre of it all, warm, clever and sparkling, is ALICE-MIRANDA. MILLIE dances up to her.

MILLIE

Merry Christmas, Alice-Miranda. This is amazing! You're amazing!

ALICE-MIRANDA

Thanks, Millie, you are too. Merry Christmas!

LUCAS and JACINTA accidentally dance into them. Oops!

JACINTA/LUCAS

Merry Christmas!

As the four friends dance together, we watch the dance floor from above, and the room slowly spins . . . a swirling feast of lights, music, ball gowns and Christmas cheer.

FADE OUT

Cast of characters

Main cast

Alice-Miranda	
Millie	One of Alice-Miranda's best friends
Jacinta	One of Alice-Miranda's best friends

Other children

Alethea	Head prefect at Winchester-field-Downsfordvale
Caprice	New student at Winchester-field-Downsfordvale
Ashima, Ivory & Susannah	Students at Winchesterfield-Downsfordvale
Lucas	Student at Fayle
Prince Edgar	Prince, student at Fayle
Prince Louis	Prince, student at Fayle

Adults

Ambrosia	Jacinta's mother
Aunt Charlotte	Alice-Miranda's aunt
Aunty Gee	Her Majesty Queen Georgiana
Bodyguard	Aunty Gee's bodyguard
Cecelia	Alice-Miranda's mother
Granny Valentina	Alice-Miranda's grandmother
Hugh	Alice-Miranda's father
Lawrence	Lucas's father
Lloyd	Aunty Gee's nephew, Marjorie's fiancé
Marjorie	Aunty Gee's head of security, Lloyd's fiancé
Miss Grimm	Headmistress of Winchester-field-Downsfordvale
Miss Higgins	Miss Grimm's secretary
Mr Lipp	Drama teacher at Fayle
Peter	Staff member on *The Queen Georgiana*
Sam	Stablehand
Tom	Popstar's trainer

Horses

Bonaparte	Alice-Miranda's pony
Popstar	Aunty Gee's prize mare
Sport	Lucas's pony

A letter from SLR Productions

Dear fellow fans,

It has been an absolute pleasure to bring a second marvellous movie with Jacqueline Harvey's awesomely positive heroine, Alice-Miranda to the screen. The first movie, *Alice-Miranda: Friends Forever*, won several awards and was screened in many countries around the world. We were so thrilled at the chance to share another of Alice-Miranda's great adventures, taking several books and turning them into an exciting royal mystery for Alice-Miranda and her friends to solve.

Making an 80-minute animated movie is a big project and we were lucky to bring back the talented writers, cast, crew and artists to help us create *Alice-Miranda: A Royal Christmas Ball*. The writers, designers, actors, storyboard artists, animators, composer, film editor, sound post, animation director, director, producers and executive producer were all once again very excited to be part of another animated movie in this popular series.

We were very lucky to have the amazing support of Jacqueline Harvey, the books' author. Alice-Miranda is her baby, and she has trusted SLR Productions on this journey. We cannot thank her enough for the guidance she has given throughout the process of making the Alice-Miranda movies. Working with Jacqueline has been an absolute delight. She is not only one of Australia's bestselling authors, but she is also one of the kindest, most positive people we know.

We can't wait for fans to see Alice-Miranda all dressed up in some of her gorgeous outfits. When we started to discuss which stories we would like to explore for the second movie, we knew her fans would love the sailor outfit and the ball dress as these were absolute fan favourites at Book Week parades and Jacqueline Harvey school visits. We instantly imagined Alice-Miranda skipping around, exploring a glamourous cruise ship, in her cute sailor dress and as a heroine riding Bony in her royal blue ball gown on a mission to save the Queen. The locations of a cruise ship and a Royal Christmas Ball seemed like a perfect follow-up to our first movie.

We had so much fun designing the ship outfits for Millie and Jacinta to go with Alice-Miranda's sweet sailor ensemble, and the gorgeous ball dresses for all the girls at Winchesterfield-Downsfordvale Academy. Creating new designs for Queen Georgiana and her best friend, Granny Valentina; the charming young princes; and, of course, the villains was all under the careful eye of Jacqueline Harvey and our talented team of artists.

Anne Yi, who is the artist who draws all the wonderful book illustrations, was once again helping us make sure we stayed true to the characters we know you all love. Bony the mischievous pony got to have his own special friendship with the Queen's favourite mare, Popstar. She was an animators' favourite, especially in the dressage competition; you will see how much fun they had animating the quirky dressage moves for the competition.

Designing the incredible *Queen Georgiana* cruise ship and researching the locations made us all want to go on a holiday, and the artists really enjoyed planning the lovely cottage and gardens of Granny Valentina, the Queen's Cup with the festive tents and the competition arena, and setting the mood for the creaky old barn in the woods.

Using the colourful and detailed locations from the first movie, we also returned to the emerald green hills surrounding the school where Alice-Miranda and her friends ride their ponies, the stables where the ponies are kept, the equestrian field, the bedrooms for midnight feasts and Fayle School for Boys. You can imagine how much fun we had decorating the grand hall for the Royal Christmas Ball and designing a giant Christmas tree full of special decorations.

We know how much Alice-Miranda and her special, heart-warming world mean to you, the audience. We know you will love *Alice-Miranda: A Royal Christmas Ball* as our favourite perpetually positive girl returns for a royal adventure full of sparkling jewels and surprising secrets.

Kindest regards,
from all the SLR Productions team
and with special thanks from the **Director** Jo Boag
and **Executive Producer** Suzanne Ryan.

Credits

Executive Producer:
Suzanne Ryan

Producers:
Suzanne Ryan
Yasmin Jones

Director:
Jo Boag

Writers:
Melanie Alexander
Alexa Moses

Storyboard Supervisor:
Ian Young

Character Design:
Anne Yi

Character Colour:
Kelly Wallwork

Model Supervisor:
Nicole Mackenzie

Background Location Design:
Peter Sheehan APDG

Location Design Colour:
Constance Chew
Michael Tomkins
Nicole Mather

Composer:
Ryan Grogan

Film Editor:
Michael O'Rourke

Sound Design:
Brendan Woithe
Declan Diacono